Catch My Breath
By Stacy Lee Lenherr

I want to thank God for getting me through this life of mine. All glory to Him. My parents are truly the most amazing people on this Earth. Without them I would have never survived. To my beautiful, smart, funny, awesome boys. May you live every day to the fullest and may you read this book when you are at least 30! To my best friend for making me laugh and helping me through the tears. And last but certainly not least to my husband. You have changed my heart and mind forever. I love your love the most.

Young and Confident

I grew up an only child. There was always this confidence I had about me. I suppose it was the way I was raised. My parents helped me to feel I could conquer the world if I wanted to, even though I had the teeth of a rattlesnake! Kids at school tried to tease me but that didn't phase me one bit. I would even wear my headgear to school knowing that the more I wore it, the faster my teeth would look beautiful.

I had lots of friends and a passion for dance! I wanted to be a dancer more than anything! I got into dance when I was 9. I met some of my best friends. We were all focused on being successful. We all got straight A's and danced 6 days a week! It was one of the best times of my life.

Through dance I got into modeling. I had been discovered by a talent manager walking through a mall in LA. I was able to do a little acting, modeling and dancing. I made a little money and even got to perform with Michael Jackson! My childhood was amazing. And I have my parents to thank for that!

And So It Begins

I met him when I was 15. We will call him Ken. I walked into drama class that first day of school, my junior year of high school. I definitely felt a spark but I couldn't explain it. I could only describe it as a moment in time where my eyes were opened wider to this person. For some reason he made an impact on me. We were instant best friends. I had a boyfriend at the time but it didn't matter. I didn't see him that way. I would say that he was like the brother I never had. We would say, "I love you" all the time. It was no big deal. Our relationship was special. I took him to my junior prom when he was a sophomore. We were just friends and we had a blast.

For about a year we were best friends. I would tell him about guys I liked and he would tell me about girls he was interested in. I remember a time when we were laying on his driveway looking at the stars. I felt happy, safe and blessed to have this great best friend. It was healthy, fun and very normal. That all began to change in the summer of 1995.

We were sitting out in his backyard on a summer night. He was laying on a lounge chair and I was cuddled up next to him on that same chair, my head on his chest. At that point I think we were both feeling more for each other but neither of us knew how to make the move. The next thing I knew he grabbed the back of my hair and brought his lips to mine. We kissed for the first time. It was very nice and certainly didn't feel like I was kissing my brother.

Our relationship was now and forever changed. We talked about how we didn't want that kiss to change us. We wanted to stay friends and keep our special relationship. It was important to the both of us. But it had changed and we would never be just friends again.

A relationship would seem to be the next step for us but it was very far from that. Summer was in full swing. I was 16 and adventurous. I met a much older guy, a professional surfer, and started dating him. Ken was very angry and I now pinpoint this as the downfall of our relationship. Ken and I still continued to hang out and share a kiss here and there. The fling with this semi-famous pro-surfer ended when school started. It was my senior year. I wanted to have fun but I was ready to try something a little more serious with Ken. One night in December 1995 I was supposed to stay the night at my girlfriend's house and instead I stayed at Ken's. His parents were gone for the night. That was the first night we were intimate. He was a virgin.

    Our relationship turned into "friends with benefits." He would get jealous if I was interested in someone and vice versa. It wasn't healthy. We barely talked anymore. We would have sex and that was it.

    I ventured out of my little circle and thought I would try dating someone new. We will call him Steven. He seemed very sweet and all was going well with him. We went on a few dates and I invited him down to my aunt's house at the beach. She had a cool place not far from the beach. She was out of town and my mom and I were taking a little vacation. I had invited Steven down, too. He could stay the night at the house but he would sleep on the couch and me in the guest room. It was important for me to take things slow. Sex can ruin a relationship if you're not ready for it. And in the teenage years with hormones raging, sex can just make things confusing and complicated. It was much better getting to know someone first. We had decided to go get some ice cream and then drive to the beach. We got out and walked to the sand. It was such a beautiful night and the waves were so loud. We started kissing and he got really worked up. I remember laughing it off to him saying, "Relax and let's just be here together." He apparently had something else in mind. He was laying on top of me. He unbuttoned my jeans and pulled them down just enough. He then pushed my underwear to the side. I told him to stop but all he kept saying was, "Come on it'll be fun." I kept saying, "No, No, Don't," but he wasn't listening. I tried to fight him off but he was too strong. It was over so quickly but felt like forever. I couldn't say anything. I got in the car and he took me back to my aunt's house. I realize now that I had probably been in shock. I walked up the stairs and locked the door behind me. Steven left. I didn't tell anyone about it. I had been raped and I ended up pregnant. I had an abortion. I wasn't sad about it. The abortion was somehow empowering. I guess for me it was saying to him that you may have done this to me, but you aren't going to change my whole life. It was an extremely traumatic event in my life. I should have gotten therapy. I didn't. I went on with my life just like nothing had happened. But it did. That event in my life changed everything for me. Steven actually tried contacting me years later to "get together for coffee," and I never responded.

    I needed something more and wanted it with Ken. He didn't want it with me and I was so fed up. I graduated that June 1996. I was ready to start fresh without him. I went to Hawaii for the summer to visit my cousin. I had a blast. I met a great older guy. We had fun. Nothing physical at all. Just fun. This older guy thought I was beautiful and funny and told me that I deserved the world. He was so sweet. I had not talked to Ken in weeks. Then as I was ready to come back home he paged me. I called him back and he said that he missed me so much and he was ready to be with me. I was so happy. Finally we would be together. He picked me up from the airport and it felt so good.

Summer of 1996 was ending and I was starting college. I had a full-time schedule and I was working as a hostess at a restaurant. I was really trying to get into the college life and focus on my future. I was spending time with my friends and having a great time.

Time started to go by and I realized I hadn't talked to Ken in a few months! One day he called me out of the blue like no time had passed at all. And we would seem to pick up where we left off. I don't know why he had such control over me but that's how it was. And I just went along with it.

For the next year we were off and on. I was a freshman in junior college and he was finishing up high school. Things between us were still so messed up. If we had only stayed friends. There was no turning back but it seemed there was no moving forward either. We went through the craziness of that year and then came summer of 1997.

My parents were having some money troubles so we ended up moving in with my aunt at the beach. It was a beautiful little community and felt like a new start for me. I enrolled in school at another junior college. I really liked it. I met some new friends and it was nice. I met a guy named Ben. I wasn't really considering dating anyone. It was really strange but even as just a girlfriend, my eyes nor my heart ever strayed from Ken. Ben became a very close friend. We studied together. We talked about everything and of course we talked about Ken. He didn't like him one bit. He would tell me that guy's bad news. In my mind I knew it but nothing could keep me from him. I told Ken about Ben and no surprise there, Ken didn't like Ben either. Ben made me a mixed tape of The Beatles. I loved it. Every time I hear The Beatles to this day I think of Ben. I wonder what happened to him? I was such a stupid girl.

My parents' financial situation improved and we ended up moving back inland. By this time I was in my second year at junior college and I had to finish up my fall semester at the junior college. I would commute to school in Orange County and drive back home for about 2 1/2 months. It really sucked driving so much but it kept me busy and thinking about the future. I would turn on the radio and get lost in the music.

Ken didn't like my short period of disconnect. He would call me often. I loved hearing from him but could feel myself moving forward with life and it felt amazing. And just like that he pulled me in once again. He was always so good at saying the right things. I was so naive that I believed him. I genuinely believed that if someone was speaking the words then they must be the truth. I guess that was because I didn't lie. So I assumed everyone else was like me. Stupid girl. That January 1998 Ken and I were on for good.

He told me that he had realized there was no other girl for him. I asked him how he knew that for sure. He so nonchalantly told me that as he was trying to have sex with a girl, that used to be my best friend, and he couldn't perform. He told me that it was at that moment he realized he was meant to be with me. Thank you??? But in my stupid 18-year-old mind I said that I was so happy he had finally figured it out and that we could really be together! What I didn't realize at the time was that Ken was clinging to me because his own family was breaking up. His mom and dad had finally decided to divorce after many years of ups and downs. He was without a place to live. The only "normal" he had in his life was me. Looking back now I realize that all those times he slept on the couch at my parent's house wasn't because he really wanted to be with me but it was because he didn't have a real place to call home.

Things actually seemed very normal for the next 6 months or so. I graduated from junior college with my AA degree. I was moving on to a University in the Fall of 1998 to study Film and TV. I was so excited. I always loved Entertainment television and I wanted to be a reporter.

Making My Way

I started school at the University. It was a lot of work but so much fun and I knew I was right where I was supposed to be. Ken spent a lot of time with me at school, assisting me on my projects and even helping with some events at school. He decided to apply with the hopes of becoming a sports reporter. At first he didn't get in. His grades were not good. I remember we had to go down to admissions and speak with a counselor about why they should accept him. I spoke on his behalf. They reluctantly agreed to go ahead with admitting him but making it very clear that he would be on academic probation and one slip up and he would be out.

I began to intern for my favorite entertainment reporter at a station in LA. He gave me some awesome confidence. He was so impressed with my organizational skills and my writing. He said I was one of the best writers he had ever had as an intern. We became very close friends. So close that his wife ended up making my wedding dress and bridesmaid dresses. I cherish that time with him. He and his wife are good quality people.

Ken had asked my dad for permission to marry me. I had told him many times how important it was to me. He asked me to marry him under the fireworks at Disneyland. We got engaged. I was 20 and he was 19. I knew it was coming I just didn't know when. On the way home from Disneyland that very important night we ran out of gas in Ken's red Chevy truck. I should've known right then and there what was to come. So young and so dumb.

    I graduated the University and started sending out tapes to stations in hopes that I would get hired for my first on-air job. I got a few bites but nothing close to home. I didn't want to leave Ken. I was supposed to be planning a wedding, getting married and hopefully starting a family. How could I go to a small town in the middle of the country now? I was told by so many..."Be an actress. Be a model. You look so young. Your voice sounds like you are 12." Ugh. I made contact with the entertainment reporter I used to intern for asking for some assistance and he helped me land my first job out of college at Columbia Pictures. I would be the Publicity Assistant for two publicists who handled TV, Radio and Newspaper media for upcoming releases for the studio. It was a crazy and interesting job. I got to meet and mingle with everyone who's anyone. While seating celebrities at the Charlie's Angels premiere, I came across who else but George Clooney. I found him his seats as he chatted me up and hit on me. But no, I was engaged. I basically said no to George Clooney! Stupid girl. In the middle of planning a wedding, I changed jobs. I thought it was time to move on. I became the personal assistant to a famous model/actress. It was another interesting experience to say the least.

Ken and I moved in together to our first place in Long Beach. It was a charming studio in the 'hood! I used to come home from work and run from my car with my key strategically placed in between my fingers like a knife! It was that scary! Once I made it inside, I wasn't scared. It was our first place and I really loved it. One night I was watching TV and I heard gunshots. They were so close that I actually ducked! I carefully looked out the window and saw some guy running down the alley. Police came to interview me but I never saw the guy's face. He shot 3 people and killed one. Ken was at work and raced home to be with me. The next day we moved out. That was quite enough of the 'hood for us! Later that day we got a call from the manager of the building saying that there had been a fire after we left and it had completely destroyed the building. Someone wanted us out of there and we were happy to be gone.

We moved to a great little studio in Huntington Beach in the same complex as a friend of mine whom I worked with at Columbia Pictures. We commuted together to LA. It was a fun and simple time.

I wasn't Bridezilla by any means. I wanted a very modest wedding of 100 people or less in a pretty location with some flowers and some food. That was it. Ken's mom and dad made it clear from the beginning that they weren't going to help out much at all. They weren't happy with us getting married so young. My parents had both explained to me that yes, they were a very happy couple but they were not the norm these days. It takes a lot of work and sacrifice to have a successful marriage. How hard could it be? Oh I had no idea. I really had no cold feet about getting married. I felt like it was the right thing to do. I trusted Ken. We had grown up together. I loved him. Whatever he said, I believed. If I had only known what was going on then. Ken and I were married in June of 2001. I was 22 and he was 21.

Married life in the beginning was very good. We were both working good jobs, making great money and building a life. He had an apprentice job at the station that I used to intern at in LA. He was great at what he did. He certainly had a face for TV and the talent to go along with. It wasn't long that while sitting on set for a lighting test as a "warm body," he was discovered by the news director. She liked his look and wanted to see what he had. The director asked Ken to look into the camera and read the prompter. He read a few lines from the latest news story of the day. She called him into his office and asked him what he was looking to do. He told her he enjoyed anchoring sports and that's what he saw himself doing. She told him he needed to be a general assignment reporter and then hopefully become an anchor. She saw big things for him and she was a great ally to have. I'll never forget when he called me and told me that story. It was amazing and would be the beginning of his career.

It wasn't long after that he would get the first call from a station in Ohio. They had received his tape and a great recommendation from the news director. He was on his way. And then September 11, 2001 would happen. Everything stopped. There would be a hiring freeze and we would have to wait. Well I guess not too long. Just two weeks after 9/11 happened, Ken flew to Ohio for his interview. It went well. Very well. Ken got the job as a general assignment reporter and we would be moving to Ohio. We had been married 4 months.

His Dreams Are Now Mine

We would move to Ohio at the end of October 2001. It was so exciting. I quit my job with the model/actress where I made 3 times as much money as Ken would now. I looked at the bigger picture. My job was to be that rock for him. A supportive wife was what I needed to be. We would miss our families but it was the beginning of our life adventure together. We had so much ahead. We loaded up my Ford Explorer Sport with our suitcases and our cat. For the next week, we spent hours and hours in the car on a road trip from California to Ohio. It was an amazing trip to take with someone you love. The soundtrack of that trip was an album by The Crash Test Dummies. Seeing the beauty of the different landscapes was a memory I will hold with me forever.

When we arrived in Ohio, the station put us up in a hotel for a few days until our townhouse was ready. Ken delayed his start date by one day since our moving van arrived late. We began to unpack and start our new life in Ohio. Ken would go to work and I would continue to unpack and make the house a home. We had only been married four months so we didn't have a lot just yet. Luckily our expenses were minimal since we were a one income family at least for now until I could find a job.

Ken had signed a 3-year deal starting at $28,000 per year. It was nothing but it was enough and we were having a blast together. It was absolutely a shock to our system being so far from our family but it seemed to be exactly what we needed to solidify the two of us as our own family. We were really happy. Life was simple.

Ken was definitely starting to make a name for himself. It was his first reporter job and he had started in a fairly big market. That was almost unheard of in those days. I was the supportive wife, never missing a live shot. We talked like best friends. We were a normal, happy and in love couple.

By May 2002, seven months after we moved to Ohio, a job as a Promotion Producer opened up at his station and it was perfect for me. I took the job and starting working upstairs. It was a great gig. I worked along side one of the most awesome women I know. She was so helpful to show me the ropes. She would become a great friend. I saw her through the planning of her wedding to an anchor at the station. She was there for me when my poor cat got sick and we had to put him down. She would also be there for me when I caught Ken in a lie that would become a pivotal part of our marriage.

Ken had also started to make some pretty good friends as well. In the news business you end up hanging out with the ones you work with. It's such a crazy business and it seems the only ones who can relate are your co-workers. I trusted Ken completely. Cheating on me was the one thing he had been most adamant about. His dad had cheated throughout the marriage to his mom. He saw what it did to her and to the family and he would always tell me that he would never do that. So knowing that, I had no qualms about him going out with co-workers after work. He worked the night shift from 2:30pm-11:30pm so often times the crew would go get a drink after the show. I worked days so that was too late for me to stay out. I never really asked questions either. I trusted him. So naive.

Surprise

Almost a year into working at the station with Ken, I got a big surprise. I had been on the pill for years. I felt sick all the time from it and so my doctor suggested a lower dose pill. One month into taking that new pill I would find out that I was pregnant. We had always said that, "Ohio was our birth control." We knew we didn't want to have kids until we were closer to our family again. Too late. It was happening now. It was a shock at first but we embraced it and knew we had 9 months to figure it all out.

While balancing my checkbook online one day at work I noticed a very, to say the least, interesting charge on our account. A charge had posted for the local strip club. My heart raced and my palms got sweaty. I couldn't believe what I was seeing. I told my co-worker right away. Her mouth was wide open. Not only had he lied but if he had been caught by someone other than me, he could get fired. There was a strict morality clause in his contract and being seen at a strip club was certainly a no no. I called him immediately. I asked him where he had gone the other night. The first thing he said was, "Why?" That would be the tell tale sign for years to come that he was lying. He asked a question instead of just giving me an answer. I asked him again. He then proceeded to tell me that he had just gone to a local bar and had a few beers. Without hesitation I said, "No you didn't. You went to a strip club. I know because I saw it on our account. Next time you try something like that and you want to keep it from me, don't use your card for our account!" I hung up. My co-worker laughed nervously and then asked if I was ok. I was so angry and upset. How could he do that and how could he lie about it? And so began the slow breakdown of trust.

After that instance of lying I began to wonder what else had he lied about. Now when he went out after work, I asked more questions. I was more suspicious. My heart wanted to trust him but my head and gut told me not to. It's amazing how that little voice in your head, that sinking feeling in your stomach, is always so right. Listen to it. I believe it's God's little way of giving you just the slightest glimpse of what's to come. A little hint. A tap on the shoulder to say, "My child, listen to me. I'm trying to save you from heartache." It's intuition and we all have it. I know it as that feeling of anxiety in my tummy telling me something is not quite right. Listen to it!

My pregnancy had been mostly easy but towards the end that baby wanted to come out early. My mom was visiting for my baby shower and the day she was supposed to leave, I went in to pre-term labor. I think it was the stress of saying goodbye that turned my body upside down. She stayed an extra week and that was great.

During all of this Ken had been getting calls from other news directors. They were trying to find another station for him. His contract stated that it was ok for him to make a move within the company during his contract. He was flown all over the place! The excitement was building because not only were we probably going to move, we were having a baby!
It was decided that Sacramento would be his next stop. He would get the morning anchor job without even having anchor experience! The company had that much faith in him. We were so excited to be moving back to California! What timing!

My beautiful baby boy was born in December of 2003. It was a snowy day in Ohio. He was perfect. I was in complete shock with how to take care of a baby. I was an only child and only babysat toddlers. Never a baby! I felt like I was in such a daze and had no idea what I was doing. Luckily my parents came to help out. I had a baby and 11 days later we would be on a plane flying to start the next chapter of our lives in Sacramento. A less than 2 week old baby, a dog and us. It was all a little too much to handle.

The company put us up in an extended stay hotel for about a week until our moving van arrived and our apartment was ready. We had seen our family for a few days when we first arrived to California. That was so nice. I didn't feel alone and I had some help with this little human being that I was now in charge of. At times I would look at my baby boy wondering if I could be all that he needed me to be. I felt very weepy and sad pretty much all the time. I was good at hiding it when other people were around. I tried to get out and about with him. The more I was at home the more sad I was. I didn't realize it at the time but I had post-partum depression and I had it bad!

So much had happened. We moved to Sacramento when our baby boy was just 11 days old. A new job, a new baby, a new life. It became too much for me. I was very depressed and not until my son was 6 months old, was I properly diagnosed with postpartum depression. I remember Ken being so mean. When he came with me to therapy he told the therapist to "fix me." She explained to him that this was a very serious condition and I needed a lot of love and support to get me through. He didn't want to have any part of that. I was put on anti-depressants and that helped.

It was during this time that Ken decided we needed a change. This behavior is something he would emulate for years to come. When things get bad or boring to him, let's disguise it with something new and exciting. So what did we do? We bought our first house! A new location, a new place to make memories for our little growing family. We painted together, picked furniture, everything. It was a new project and is distracted Ken for just a little bit. But not for too long.

The First Affair:
Ego Takes Over

She actually befriended me. She was his co-anchor. I really liked her. She helped me make curtains for my house. We got pedicures together. We went to the movies.

I remember feeling in my gut that something just wasn't right. I didn't like the way he talked to her. I didn't like the way they fought. There was too much passion. A work wife she was not. I knew something was up when I found him huddled in our closet talking to her on the phone. I asked him what was going on. He explained with a shocked look on his face that it was her and that she and her husband were having problems. "Why is that your problem?" I thought to myself, but never said it out loud.

Our sex life continued as normal. That was never a problem for us. In fact, it was probably the strongest part of our relationship.

And then so it began. We were at dinner one night with his mom who came to town to visit. He got a phone call. It was her and he had to take it. He got up from the table and walked away. His mom and I looked at each other and without saying a word, we both knew what was happening. He came back from his phone call with her and he was frazzled. His mom questioned him and he snapped at her. Something was up but I had no idea the extent of it all.

That Monday at work he was called in to the GM's office. His co-anchor was not on the desk with him that day. He came out of the office and straight to my office. I had taken on a job at the station as well as a promotion producer. He told me that his co-anchor was telling his bosses that she could no longer work with Ken because he was abusive and that their affair could no longer continue. What? He assured me that she was crazy and that the only reason she was accusing him of all of this was because he denied her advances and she was angry. I actually believed him.

A few days later I wasn't feeling well and my period was late. I took a test in the bathroom at work. It was positive. I was pregnant with our second child. It should have been a very happy time. It wasn't. I had a feeling in my stomach that had nothing to do with the life growing inside of me. It was confusion and helplessness. I had no idea what was next but I just wanted it to be over.

The very next day my world would come crashing down. I was home getting ready for work when there was a knock at the door. It was his co-anchor's husband. I didn't answer it. With everything I had been told, it felt like I was now being harassed. The husband was insisting, through the door, that my husband and his wife had indeed been having an affair. I told him to go away. I called Ken immediately to tell him that all of this had to stop. He needed to come home right now and we needed to march right into his bosses office to end this thing once and for all.

Ken came home to get me. He consoled me. He told me it was all going to be alright, but that couldn't have been further from the truth. In the car on the way back to the station he was very nervous. I will never forget. He kept drinking from this water bottle. Every time he would pick it up he would sort of throw it up in the air and catch it. It seemed strange and annoying and it sticks out in my mind to this day. Halfway to the station he proceeded to tell me that he and his co-anchor had indeed had an affair. I began to cry and told him it was over. I would leave and take our son. I was pregnant but that didn't matter. I would take care of myself. He cried to me and begged me not to go. "Please give me another chance. I'm sorry," he said. As we pulled up to the station he explained that his bosses knew of the affair and that he had confessed to them about it. He said that he had told them that I knew everything and that I was fine with it all. Fine with it all? Really? We walked in to his bosses office and there the big charade unfolded. I played it like the actress I had become. Yes, I knew about the affair and we are working on things. I said that I was now pregnant and thrilled with the idea of adding to our family. I told them that I would appreciate them telling the co-anchor's husband to leave me alone and that in my delicate state I certainly didn't need him harassing me. I knew using words like "harass" isn't something a big company wants to hear. The bosses said that the co-anchor would not be returning. She would be moving back to her hometown to a take a new job. How nice for her.

    I was dying inside. I left that office feeling so dirty like I had been the one to have the affair. I felt myself changing and I didn't like it one bit. But what do I do now? I'm pregnant. My husband's job is in jeopardy. I have to be the glue that holds this wounded family together right? It was my duty to at least try to fix this. I was so wrong. I walked to my desk and carried on at work as if my world wasn't crumbling. That was the beginning of learning to put on a show.

I cried so many times. My heart was breaking a little bit every single day. I went to work. I smiled. I did my job. I didn't even tell my friends or my family what was happening. It's hard to imagine unless you are in it. I always told myself that I would never stand for cheating. But then you start to question whether or not this was all my fault. Crazy but that's what you do. It was during that hard time I was having with postpartum depression, that the affair with the co-anchor began. He told me that he had looked to her for strength because I had become so weak. And I had become weak. Weak because I had a spouse that didn't value me anymore. Instead of loving me through the hard times, he loved himself instead. He didn't realize that I had given up my dreams to support his. My new dream had become his career and this family. What would I have left now? I loved my husband to a fault. I began to love him much more than I loved myself. Deep down I thought if I could just love him enough he would see and then everything would be ok. I should have walked away. That first affair should have been the last if I had just walked away. That's what I should have done. But I stayed. I stayed way too long.

I think when your husband cheats on you, you really want to think it was a weak moment and it will never happen again. But I learned, it usually does. I know some marriages can recover but only if the cheater really feels remorse and wants to change. After that first affair, or at least what I thought was the first affair, I kept thinking about that phrase, "Once a cheater, always a cheater." Could it be different for my husband? Was it just one weak time in his life? How could I ever fully trust him again? The answer to all of those questions was, no.

My pregnancy with my second child was so rough. I had contractions, bleeding and went into pre-term labor at 4 months along. It was when I was in the hospital for complications that we found out the sex of our second child. The tech so nonchalantly said, "So your baby boy looks like he's doing just fine." What? We didn't even want to know. Thanks a lot! I was put on "modified" bed rest because I did after all, have a toddler to care for. My emotions were so up and down. My belly was growing and I was so unhappy. I was dying inside. Why didn't I have a husband who loved me and cared for me like I deserve? I was a good person, mother, and wife. What was wrong with me? He never cared to enjoy the amazing moments of the baby moving nor did he ever want to feel my belly. There was no attachment to me or to the baby. It was all about him and as long as he was happy, life in our home was good. I lost myself in that. His needs were put first, even before my children and of course, before myself.

Baby Blues

With the birth of my second son in September of 2005 came another traumatic and life-changing event. Everything seemed to go so well with the birth which was such a contrast to the entire pregnancy. He was born in 4 hours and he was beautiful. He was perfect. A little too perfect. We brought him home from the hospital and he was just too quiet. He ate fine, slept great, and all of his parts seemed to be working just fine. He hardly cried. It didn't feel right to me. His color was a little off, too. A little jaundiced but the nurses told me it would pass. At just 3 days old my perfect little baby boy stopped breathing. He was laying right next to me as I was pumping my breasts. I looked over at him one minute and he was fine and the next he was purple. I said, "Oh my God!" My mother-in-law, was staying with us and she jumped up and ran to the phone to call 911. I remember throwing down the pump and picking up my baby boy so fast. It's as if I floated above my body and couldn't believe what was happening. I remember a voice inside of me wanting to scream and cry but another voice being calm and telling me exactly what to do. I started breathing into his tiny little mouth while covering his nose. I was holding him in the air and on his back. I kept saying calmly, "Come on baby, come on." There was no response from him. He was lifeless and purple. I was losing my baby. I had tears running down my face. The 911 operator finally came on the line after being on hold for what seemed like an eternity. In between breaths my mother-in-law would ask me my address, phone number and cross streets so that the paramedics could get to us. I would calmly tell her everything. I even told her to put the dog outside so she would be safe and confined to the backyard while all of this chaos was happening around us."Put him on the floor flat on the ground and raise his chest," she told me. I started the breaths again. I did the compressions on his tiny little chest. I finally heard the sound I was longing to hear. A slight faint cry from my poor baby boy. I started crying more and still doing breaths. "Police department, Police department," I heard a man say while he ran in my house. Probably the biggest and tallest man I had ever seen. He ran over to me and my baby. "Oh Thank God!" He said. The officer was so happy to see my little guy alive and told me that he was so worried about doing CPR on such a tiny infant.

After that, the fire department showed up along with the paramedics.

The paramedics took my baby from me and assessed him. I got up from the ground and my shirt was soaked with breast milk. It was my college t-shirt. The officer sweetly and quietly suggested that maybe I would want to change for the ride to the hospital. I quickly did and off we went. On the way to the hospital my baby boy stopped breathing again. Something was very wrong but what? He was rushed to the local Children's Hospital. He was put on a bed and immediately looked at by ER staff. He was wrapped in warm blankets and his temperature was taken. It was 93 degrees F. My baby boy was dying. The ER doc scooped him up in his arms and put him in his own room and bed. He was so little laying on this huge hospital bed. The alarms kept going off. His body wanted to die and he kept losing his breath. Finally Ken arrived. He had been out with our older son and got the call from his mom that something was very wrong. He had dropped off our older son and raced to the hospital. I remember his eyes being red like he had been crying but the look on his face was that of blame. I felt like he was saying, "What did you do?" He never asked me if I was ok or comforted me. My baby boy was quickly moved to the NICU where he was evaluated by the best doctors around. We were up all night. Finally around 6am I called the family to tell them what had happened and they all made the trek up to see us.

   I was at the hospital day and night. I continued to pump breast milk at home, even in the middle of the night in hopes that my boy would soon get to enjoy a normal life and need the best of me. It was touch and go for those first few days but those doctors finally figured out he had a blood infection. It was a bad bug called Enterobacter aerogenes. In the bacteria world it was considered a cousin to E coli. I did my research. It was bad and he had survived. It can never be proven how he got this blood infection at just 3 days old but all of my research points to dirty hospital equipment when he was first born. He would be given a series of strong antibiotics. For the first few days I couldn't even hold him. He was hooked up to machines with wires everywhere and under these high powered lamps to keep his temperature up. It was a miracle that he had survived. Doctors told me it truly was a miracle. Most adults would have died.

   I remember when the nurse called to tell us that we could come and hold him and feed him. I screamed with joy, cried, and got right in the car to get to the hospital. Just to enter the NICU we had to put on scrubs and scrub our hands all the way up to our elbows. It felt amazing to hold him. All I wanted to do was snuggle with him and love him like I had wanted to do everyday since he was born. But it was serious business. If he was ever going to get to come home he had to show them that he was progressing normally and eating. With the nurse's help we first tried to allow him to latch on and breast feed. It seemed all he wanted to do was snuggle, too. Once he was in my arms and against my chest, all he wanted to do was sleep. I had been longing for that for so long that I didn't mind but the nurses weren't having it! They took him from me and gave him a bottle of my breast milk. They rubbed his head vigorously to keep him awake. By the third day of this he had gotten the hang of it and I was able to feed him and keep him awake. Progress was being made. He was getting so much stronger, gaining weight and almost ready to come home.

After 16 days in the hospital I brought my baby home. I was so happy. My focus had been turned to our child and Ken didn't like that. He would never admit it but he hated the attention being taken off of him even for the sake of our children. He was sick. I never understood but I always catered to his needs. I thought I was doing my very best by being the most amazing wife I could be. I was trying

like hell to put all of my efforts into
making our family whole again. I got
lost again and that didn't last long.

Again and again

I became very suspicious of Ken. He would be on his phone and on the computer constantly. When I would come into the room he would stop what he was doing. I knew something was up. Around Thanksgiving I started looking at phone records. I noticed a time where he said he was going to be one place and was somewhere completely different. I called a few numbers and got to the bottom of what I knew I would find. A girl named Karina answered and I told her who I was. She explained to me that she had met Ken on a weekend in Palm Springs. Ken had told her that he was getting a divorce. I asked her what happened between them and she was honest. They'd had sex. At the time this had happened I was 9 months pregnant and it was my baby shower weekend. Unbelievable. I was devastated. I called him and told him what I had found out. He yelled at me and hung up. And I took it. I know, you will never understand until you live it. I wasn't me anymore. I didn't know how to be me. The alternative of learning how to be me again was scary. This was my new normal, although completely wrong and so messed up, normal.

All this time I should have been gone. I should have been enjoying my beautiful boys and living life without him. This wasn't living at all. This was coping. And what do we do when things are rough? We decided to move and start fresh in a new home. We went out and bought new furniture for this huge new home. It was fun fixing it up but once that part was over, it was lonely and I saw that Ken's tricks were continuing. We started to get phone calls from a lot of different 800 numbers. I would answer the calls and then Ken told me to stop and ignore them, so I did. He told me that his identity had been stolen and he was handling it. I believed him. Just days after that conversation he came home and said that we needed to talk. He said that he had gambled and gotten in for more that he could pay. In a very mattter-of-fact way he tells me that we need to sell my engagement ring. What? He said that's the only way we can get guaranteed cash now. For some reason I just went along with it. We put the boys in the car and headed out to sell my ring. Just like that I didn't have my one carat solitaire that had been so simple and so beautiful. He vowed that he would get me a new one just as soon as our money issues improved. I believed him.

One weekend Ken took the boys to Southern California for the weekend while I stayed behind. I had a bunch of projects in our new home and welcomed the alone time. I must say looking back, I had something else on my mind as well. I got stuff done around the house and decided to go out with a girlfriend. Her boyfriend had a friend in town visiting and we would all go out for drinks. In my mind I knew what I would do. I would get revenge and there was only one way how. I remembered my mother-in-law telling me that for every time my father-in-law cheated on her she would go out and do it to him. A sick way to live, but in a way I understood. It didn't take long to cozy up to the friend and from there it all just happened. I cheated on my husband that night. It wasn't right but at the time it felt like what I needed and wanted to do. I will always regret that night. I still do. It's not who I am but then again, who was I?

Everything was fun for a little while in our new home but once the newness wore off, things were worse and now he was getting physical. I tried so hard to keep things as happy as possible for the boys. He would come home and get on the computer or his phone and I would ask him who he was talking to. He would yell at me. I would tell him to stop yelling and he would push me away or grab me. I bruise easily so I would have bruises and marks on my arms all the time. The final straw was when he was yelling at me and my oldest son told him to "stop making Mommy cry." The next morning I packed up a few things and took the boys down to Southern California to stay with my parents.

    Ken called me a few days after we left to say that he had found out that I had cheated on him that night. He said that it was over. I had cheated. How could I do that? I felt awful. I was not a cheater and that was certainly not who I wanted to be. I reminded him of the times he had cheated on me. That didn't matter. This was my fault and I would have to live with that. My life as a wife was over. Who would I be now? What would I do with my life now? My identity was gone. I had no idea who I was anymore.

The Healing

When my boys and I moved in with my parents they were 3 1/2 and 1 1/2. I felt like such a loser. I basically stopped eating and survived mostly on Starbucks and granola bars. I lost almost 30lbs almost immediately. I was so unhealthy.

The first few months were such a blur. I remember my best friend Taylor coming over to see me. I was skinny, my face was broken out and my eyebrows needed some serious waxing. She looked at me and said, "I like this new look you have goin' on!" We both laughed. I needed that so much! I was starting to find the humor in it all. She helped to bring me back.

My mom took me to Hawaii for my 29th birthday. I remember feeling so good and so free there. But the minute I started to let go and heal, he would text me to say that he missed me. I would go back and forth wondering what I should do.

I decided to go to Esthetician school and start a new career. The school and the girls there were such an amazing help to bringing me back to me again. I was having girl time and learning at the same time. It was there that I met my first crush after Ken. He was just about the only cute guy in a school full of girls. I thought about how great it would be to go out with him but I was an almost 30 year-old single mom. What would he possibly see in me? Well, he saw something and we started dating. It felt so great to be the girl that he wanted to be with. He was so different from Ken. He had tattoos! It was fun and it made me forget about Ken.

I got my Esthetician's license, got a job and moved into my very own place with the boys! I was getting to go out with my friends who said they had missed me so much. I was getting into great shape, eating right and feeling so good.

Ken had mismanaged our money so much. With gambling debts, credit card debt and other unpaid bills, our best move was to file for bankruptcy.

It seemed that we were both moving on with our lives. Ken had a new girlfriend. I was dating. It was great. But things always seem to change. Ken and his girlfriend broke up. My business closed and I lost my job. I wasn't dating that guy anymore and nothing was on the horizon. I felt stuck and didn't know what was next. Ken and I were both in low places and we were weak for each other. We began talking about memories. Only good ones of course. We would talk about silly things and situations. We were both longing for something familiar and we found that in each other. We had been separated for a year. We decided to get back together. I moved back to Sacramento with the boys.

Let The Games Begin

Things seemed to be good now that we were all together again. Money wasn't so tight anymore since we had combined bills. The kids seemed happy. Life seemed good again. It felt like the right decision. Not long after we moved back, I was in our closet hanging up clothes. I remember being on the phone with him and it felt like he was up to his old tricks again. He had made up some excuse as to why he wouldn't be home right away after work. I questioned him and he made me feel that all too familiar way that it was all my fault. I started to cry, staring at all of our things wondering what I had done. Out loud I said, "Is this happening again?" Had I made a bad decision getting back together with him?

    We were only in Sacramento for 3 months when his contract there was up and he was offered a job at a news station in Los Angeles. It was his dream, and mine, to go back to LA where it all started and to be close to family. To think our dreams were coming true and we were a family again was amazing. I still felt so much doubt and dread inside of me. I could never relax because deep down inside of me I knew all of this would come crashing down again. Not a good way to live. I used to be so optimistic but now I was becoming realistic. I remember being at his going away party and all of these past flings of his were there. Some had been with him while we were married and some had gotten at him while we were separated. I tried not to think too much of it. Instead I thought of him as the prize that I had won. He had decided to be with me. I was so lucky. Some prize...

We moved to LA. He started out on weekends and quickly was noticed and put in the anchor chair as the main anchor! He wasn't even 30 and he was the main anchor at a legendary station in the #2 market in the country! Wow! I was so proud of him. I was cheering for him every step of the way. But, as I know all too well, good times never last too long.

He started to go out after the evening show. He would go to a local bar with the crew and producers. I didn't mind it once in awhile, but it started to happen several nights a week. One night after he got home after a night out I snuck and looked at his phone. I found exactly what I thought I would find. Texts and calls from many women. Completely inappropriate texts for a married man. I questioned him but he told me I was crazy and he didn't care what I had to say. He had called

one of his colleague's "stunning." To
this day, I hate that word.

Model Behavior

The breakdown of our marriage, again, went very quickly from there. I left for a weekend with the boys and knew I couldn't do this anymore. He called me while I was away and told me that he needed to see me. I left the boys with my parents and took the hour drive wondering what in the world he was going to say. I got to our home and he greeted me with a hug and tears. He told me that he couldn't do this anymore. He said that he knew that I deserved better. What? These were words he had never spoken before. Why now? During this intense conversation he was on his phone a lot. Annoyed, I asked him who could he possibly be talking to at a time like this? He said that I would never believe him and that this person was part of the reason he was leaving me. Strangely enough I was very calm. He told me that he was communicating with a famous musician, who was friends with this new woman in his life. He told me that she was a famous model in London and that they had been speaking for about a month. She had reached out to him through the news station's website. I asked him how they had been communicating. He told me it was by email and that they had spoken on the phone a few times. For some reason, my first question to him was, "How do you know that she is even real?" He laughed and said of course she is. I asked him, for my peace of mind, why don't you find an email address for her publicist and email him/her to find out if that indeed is her personal email address. He said that he would. We both agreed that we would take some more time to decide what would be next for us. My parents brought the boys back to us and I shared a little of our conversation. They were furious and couldn't believe he was doing it all over again. I was exhausted but couldn't sleep.

My fears were confirmed later that next day when the real publicist wrote back to say that he was afraid that the email address was not hers and that it appeared that he had been speaking with an imposter. "I'm afraid that's not her personal address. Good luck to you," the publicist said. That would be the understatement of the century and so would begin one of the most unbelievable times in our lives.

I'm still not sure if I know the whole truth to this next part and I probably never will but here's how I knew it all to be. One email seemed to change Ken's mind that day. This so-called famous model's very real publicist had given Ken the news that he had been communicating with a fraud. Who had he been emailing and speaking with? Ken became very angry and emailed both the "famous model" and "famous musician" to say that he knew they were fakes. Their tone both quickly changed as well. The witty banter he had shared with the musician had now turned into very threatening words towards Ken and our family. The loving sweet talk he had been sharing with the model, now became very hostile. She began to say things like, "I know where your kids go to school" and "What if something were to happen to your wife?" It all became so scary so fast. "The musician" was very angry and threatened to go to his work and expose all of the emails and talk the two had communicated. It was all guys being guys but some of it was raunchy and all of it had been done through work email. I begged Ken to call work and explain what had happened before this person followed through with his threats but Ken assured me he would handle it once he got in to work the next afternoon. I also begged for him to call the police because we were all being threatened but he didn't want to.

Needless to say that first night I barely slept. I felt so scared and vulnerable. What had he told these strangers? About our boys? About me? Were they right outside our window? Were they watching us? Did they know our patterns? Would they hurt the boys? Were they crazy enough to kill us? It was awful. I just wanted it to be light outside. Even though I was exhausted, the light was much better than the dark. Ken had no trouble sleeping.

We talked that morning. He said everything would be ok. He told me how thankful he was for me sticking by him. That I was a saint and that I just never give up. That afternoon, Ken went off to work and I was scared out of my mind. We lived in a beautiful home near the foothills of Glendale. A charming multi-million dollar home with floor to ceiling windows everywhere and no security system. I was afraid for my life and my children's. What had he done and who were we dealing with? Before I could think too much Ken was calling me telling me he was on his way home. "The musician" had indeed sent some rather nasty emails that the two had shared to just about every important person at his station! As soon as he got into work he was called in to discuss it all. Ken told me that they had all agreed that he needed to be on paid leave while the company investigated the whole thing. They told us that due to the threats we should call the police. Ken called the police and made a report.

One day, there was a woman parked outside our house but across the street. She was sitting there calmly reading a book. I had noticed her before and thought nothing of it. I called the police and they came immediately. They questioned her and let her go.

We waited and waited for some word from the station about their investigation. After an appointment with a sex therapist, an apparent PR attempt to save his job, 3 weeks after "the musician" sent those emails, Ken was being asked to resign. After several meetings with bosses and station higher ups, none that I was allowed to attend, Ken was out a job. I was told that the company couldn't take any of these emails that were extremely sexual in nature, coming out about their trusted main anchor. What now? How could he recover from this? How would he support our family? Who was this crazy person on the other end of those emails? That last question should have been the most important question answered first!

In those very first days that followed Ken resigning there was so much fear, dread and anger. What had he done? How could he be so stupid? So gullible? He was a reporter. Wasn't that his job to find out the truth? His ego was so big. He truly believed this is the sort of thing that happens to the main anchor in LA. His ego was bruised but he almost immediately started looking into jobs. We tried to carry on like a normal family. I would take the kids to school everyday and sometimes he would come with me. We would go to the gym, have lunch, very normal things. I did tell the school about this possible threat of a stalker. The personas had said some very threatening things. Everywhere I went I looked around wondering if we were being watched. I imagined it was some huge, scary chick that could definitely hurt me or my family.

Strange things happened. One night I couldn't sleep and I got up for a change in scenery. In the middle of the hallway there was a blanket folded up just sitting there. The blanket had been in a box in our downstairs guest bedroom. How did it get into the hallway? My dog was violently throwing up and had uncontrollable diarrhea one day. Had she poisoned my poor dog? It was a terrible way to live not knowing who this crazy person was.

I became completely obsessed with finding this person who had ruined our lives. I stayed up all night researching on the computer. I looked at just about every article that had been written about Ken regarding his resignation. There were blogs that talked about him being a sexual predator. There was mention of Ken assaulting a co-worker in the parking lot at the station. The bloggers even said that the assault had been recorded on security cameras. I asked Ken about all of it. He swore to me that it was the stalker continuing her ambush on him and his career. I believed him.

We went on with life. The biggest priority seemed to be finding a new job. The money was dwindling down. His parents were helping us a little bit. After all, it was their son who had caused this damage. They paid the kids school tuition, helped with groceries but very soon the decision had to be made. Ken's agent had been very helpful and motivational. Their office was behind Ken and they would find him a job.

A Second Chance?

Ken actually made contact with a news director in Colorado. She really liked him for this Business Anchor job. He had never done that before but it wasn't stopping him. Ken was very forthcoming with her about what had happened at the LA station. She insisted that she and the higher ups would protect him from anymore "attacks." After weeks of talking and negotiating Ken took the job as a business anchor in Colorado. We packed up our home and moved it to storage. The boys and I would stay behind In California until after Christmas so that they could finish out the calendar year at their school. We would stay with friends and family until we moved to Colorado. Sounds like a fresh new start, right? Not so fast.

It was my oldest son's birthday in December 2009. Ken had been training for 2 weeks and would finally be on the air today. It went great! He was so happy to be back doing what he loved. I was very proud that he could have that back. In less than 24 hours the "stalker" struck again. Emails were sent to employees at his new station in Colorado just like they had been sent to LA. His bosses called him in to discuss what would be next. They took him off the air for a day and that one day turned in to forever. Another job would be lost to this whole situation. You have got to be kidding me? What now?

    Just two days after he made his debut on the air, he was on a plane back to California. The boys and I had been staying with my parents. It was supposed to be only for a month but it was looking like indefinitely. I picked him up from the airport. I was not happy to see him under these circumstances. I cried when he stepped into the car. I asked him, "How could this happen again?" He was mad at me. "He said, "I didn't do anything wrong!" I told him that if he hand't been so stupid in the first place we would never be here! I was so angry and beyond frustrated. What had he done to all of our lives? What would be next? We both agreed that this crazy person had to be found and stopped.

You Can't Write This Stuff

It took only a few days and we were in the office of an attorney who was an expert on cyber crime. He told us that by analyzing this case he would expect to find this person in 3-6 months and all would be well. Really? He said that we needed to be patient. Getting cell phone records, email records, IP addresses, etc took time. It wasn't like CSI. There were the appropriate legal channels we had to go through and laws to follow to get this thing done right. After a month of hearing next to nothing we finally got a call from the attorney. He told us that he had a friend in the FBI that could maybe help us along with our case. He would have to sort of "pitch" the case to them and hope that they would want to investigate. Finally after about another month they decided to take on the case. Ken met with them, without me, and things began to move. He told me that the special agent only wanted to meet with him because of privacy issues. I believed him.

    During this "down" time Ken looked for jobs everywhere. He went on sales job interviews. He applied at Costco. He even took some steps in becoming a firefighter. He had begun to give up that he would never be on TV again. I took on a job working with the 2010

Census while he took on the role of stay-at-home dad.

We retained an attorney to see what could be done about his remaining contract in Colorado. They really had no grounds to fire him so we fought that pretty hard. Within a couple of weeks we reached an agreement with the Colorado station and moved on.

We were talking one day about how crazy this all was and how it would make for a great news story. I suggested he contact a former co-worker from the LA station who now worked for a network in NY to see if there was anything he could do or help. Ken had interned for him at the station in LA when this guy was a local sports anchor. Ken emailed him right then and there and within an hour, he wrote back! He said that he was in the Amazon at the moment but would definitely be interested in helping us and getting this story out! It was the break we needed! Maybe Ken could finally clear his name and this crazy person would be caught?

Producers for a network news show came out to California to interview us and to follow us around in our daily lives. By this time we had moved out into our own home thanks to my salary with the Census and an "agreement" we had reached with the station in Colorado. Cameras followed us as we took the boys to school as we ate dinner, etc. They happened to be in town shooting when Ken got a very important call from the FBI. There was news. Big news.

The next day we would all caravan down to the FBI offices in Long Beach, CA. We were nervous and excited. We hoped they were going to tell us that they had found the woman that had caused all of this. The woman that had turned our world upside down. Ken went in alone, of course. I waited across the street in the van with the producer and photographers from the network. They wanted him to tell me the news first on camera. We waited. Not too long later, I got the call from Ken. He was ready to be picked up to meet me to tell me the news. I tried to listen to his voice to hear any indication of the news but I really couldn't tell. He came walking up towards me, cameras rolling. What I was about to hear I never expected. I still don't know to this day if Ken knew what was coming. Ken sits down on the steps and proceeds to tell me the story of how the meeting went with the FBI. He said that they sat him down and showed him a piece of paper with 6-8 faces on it. The special agent asked him if any of the faces looked familiar. He said one of the faces looked a little like a guy he went to junior high school with but he couldn't be sure. He didn't recognize any of the others. Ken, confused by now since all of the faces were males, asked the question that appeared to be the elephant in the room. "Who are these guys? Why are you showing me pictures of guys? The person I was communicating with was a woman. I spoke to her a few times." The special agent told him that the person they tracked down and were pinning all of this on, was indeed a man. "What the fuck are you talking about?" Ken said. "I spoke to a woman." The special agent told Ken that the man they believe to be the person who did this to him, his career, his family and his marriage, was a man with a very high voice. He could have easily been mistaken for a woman on the phone. Ken immediately felt sick to his stomach. But that wasn't all. This man was claiming that he and Ken had a sexual relationship and he had Ken's DNA to prove it! Ken obviously denied any of that. The special agent then asked if Ken would submit to a DNA test to rule him out as the person whose DNA this man had. He agreed and they swabbed his cheek. Ken asked the special agent, "What now?" He said that they had a very serious conversation with the man. The special agent assured Ken that the man would not be going after Ken or our family ever again. Ken asked him how he could be so sure. The special agent kept insisting that the man would stay away and never do any of this again. Ken was in shock and didn't ask many of the appropriate questions we were all dying to know. How could the special agent be so sure? Was the man dead? Did they take his computer away? Was he in jail? Was he deported? There were no arrests made and at that point we were supposed to be satisfied. No way!

    Ken was able to ask some of those questions to the special agent the next day. The special agent couldn't tell him how he was so sure but he was sure that this man would never bother him or us again. The next step was now seeing if the US Attorney's office would file formal charges against the man given all of the evidence that the FBI had collected. That wait would be another month or so. The call came from the special agent. No, there would be no charges filed. The US Attorney's office felt it was the case of a "lovers quarrel" gone very bad. What? My husband in a lovers quarrel with another man? You can't be serious. Again, I don't know if it really was or wasn't. At this point in my life, nothing would surprise me.

    So there it was. The MAN had been found but not arrested. The nightmare seemed to be over but there was still so much to repair. In the months while we waited for news from the FBI, Ken and I had our ups and downs. Ken would do odd jobs here and there for money. He was a drummer so he joined a local band and played gigs around town. We didn't have much but it felt like we were really close. I felt like he was being a good husband and a good father. I mean what else could he do, right? It seemed that he was putting the effort in to our family and it felt great. It looked as though things were really looking up. One day, while we were at our son's baseball game, Ken got the most amazing call from his agent. A station in Florida was interested in Ken for a position! Florida? I hated Florida! But, it was a job and he couldn't be too picky now. That call was in May of 2010.

Ken was feeling better and so our family was, too. When he was happy, we all were. We had a great summer. We spent most of our time together as a family. I felt like I had the husband I had always wanted in Ken. We weren't fighting and things felt very peaceful. It seemed to be the perfect decision to renew our vows. We decided to renew them with just the four of us on our 9th wedding anniversary. It was June 16, 2010. My very good friend took our pictures and the crew from the network was there to film it all. We were such a happy family. It felt amazing.

You Can Only Take So Much

I was having lunch with a good friend one day telling her about the latest in the saga of our lives. Despite all of the drama I felt pretty happy. We were laughing and carrying on when all of a sudden I felt the strangest feeling. My ears started to ring and my eyes got blurry. My heart started to race and I felt as if I was going to pass out. My friend asked me immediately what was wrong. I told her I didn't know. My face went white and I just put my head down and closed my eyes. She asked the waitress for a Coke and I drank it. Turns out it was a panic attack. I had never had one of those before and I never wanted to have one again! But I would have them again and again.

    I went to the doctor, to a clinic, because we didn't have insurance. I told the doctor all of my symptoms and she agreed. They were indeed panic attacks brought on by Post-Traumatic Stress Disorder (PTSD). She said that with all of the stress I had been under for the last few years, my body could no longer take anymore. She said that my best bet was to try and stay out of stressful situations and remain as calm as possible. Just about any small stress could trigger a panic attack. It was awful. The doctor prescribed me Xanax. The panic attacks would happen while being in a crowded store or while driving on the freeway. If the shoulder was closed on the freeway I would have to find the next exit and get off immediately. If I ever felt, "trapped" that's when an attack would happen. The only time I felt, "normal" was when I took half a Xanax. I try to stay away from Xanax and any prescription drugs now. The panic attacks continued for many years and still happen once in awhile to this day. I wouldn't wish one on my worst enemy. Well maybe there are a couple of people I could think of...

Despite my personal setbacks, things just kept getting better. Ken got the call from the Florida station that they wanted to fly us both out for his interview. That was a very good sign that the station was very serious about hiring Ken. We were so happy. On the way to the airport, Ken got a call from his old news director in LA. There was going to be an opening for an anchor and they were considering hiring him back. It had been over a year since he had been on the air. Ken had shared the news with old co-workers that the stalker had been caught and there was no longer a threat to him. We were literally at the airport ready to fly to Florida when that call came! Ken told his old news director that of course he would love to come back. He told him that he was headed to Florida for a very promising job interview and if they really wanted him back then they needed to act fast.

We flew to Florida that day in early October 2010. It was a great trip. The GM and his wife showed us around, took us to dinner. It was awesome. I could see myself living there. We both couldn't help talking over and over about the prospect of LA station. How great to be able just to go back. Could we have our life back again? Well, not completely the old life but a new one with the old job and money? It was something to think about. Did we really want to take our family 3,000 miles away? Our whole family lived in California. We knew that we had to consider Florida for sure. They had been the ones who had kept the dream alive for Ken to get back on the air. They had been so patient and amazing with the FBI investigation. Our loyalty right now was to Florida. The LA station had left him in the dust when everything went down. Both jobs were something to think about.

We flew back to California and decided to stay in LA with hopes of meeting with the station. We waited around all day. The call finally came as we were in the car on our way back home to pick up our boys. The LA station was interested but couldn't act quickly. We had already been stalling the Florida station. Could we afford to wait and see what LA would decide? After a long talk together and with our family, we decided that Florida was the job he would take.

    We moved out of our house in November and in to my parent's to save some money while Ken began work in Florida. Those first few days on the air were nerve-racking. Would the stalker strike again? Would he be out another job if he did? I came up with a name for the stalker. I so lovingly called him Crazy Balls.

    Ken's job in Florida was going very smoothly. They really seemed to like him there. He was so happy to be back on the air doing the job that he loved and that he was so good at. I didn't once think about not trusting him while he was in Florida those first couple of months alone. I was that confident in us. He was staying in a studio apartment until we could find the house that we really wanted. He came out to visit for our son's birthday and for Christmas. Things were good. Life seemed to be moving in the right direction, for him, for us and for our family. In January 2011, we found our perfect house and Ken moved in. Ken flew out to California to pick us up and begin our road trip across the country. He even worked it out as a story for his station. We took a week to drive across the country. Every stop we would make Ken would Skype live on the air. It was a great trip with our family. Even our little mini doxie enjoyed the ride. We took video of it all and will cherish that trip forever. On the last day of our trip we arrived at our new home in Florida. A camera crew was waiting as we pulled up. We were so happy to be together. So happy to be continuing the dream that we had for our family. Ken was so happy to have us there. He kept saying to me, "Now that you are here this finally feels like a home." That was January 2011.

Things remained quiet and we wondered what would become of the network news story. They had done so much work on it. Coming out to us and flying us to NY for the interview. It was so important to me that people new the truth of what had happened. I of course wasn't in on the conversation but the reason that was given to me as to why the network decided not to air the story was because Ken and our family were safe now and they didn't want to "shake the beehive." I was frustrated with that but moved on. Years later I tried contacting the producer to see if she would talk to me but I got no response. I will probably never know the real reason.

I began the unpacking and putting pictures up on the walls. The boys started school. My oldest was continuing 1st grade and my little guy, pre-school. All just seemed to fall in line so beautifully. The boys made friends and so did I. We became very involved in local charities and ones near and dear to our hearts like the Alzheimer's Association. We felt like members of a community. Both boys kicked butt at baseball and had so much fun. We did so much together. Baseball games, vacations, dinners, etc. We really did seem to have it all. It was a dream come true. I was more attracted to my husband than ever. There was nothing sexier than a man who loved his wife. My husband was loving me and it felt like I was on top of the world. Yep, you guessed it. Not so fast. Don't get too comfortable in the happiness for hell is just around the corner.

Breaking News: Breakdown

In the summer of 2011 we decided that I would take the boys to California for 6 weeks. We would see the family, visit with friends and enjoy life and relief from the Florida humidity. I felt confident and comfortable in my marriage that I could do this. I knew we would be just fine. He was after all, a changed man, right? About two weeks into our trip to California, something didn't feel right. Ken was a little distant and I felt that familiar feeling that he wasn't doing right by me. He came to visit and we took a little vacation to Pelican Hill with his mom and our boys. His mom noticed it, too. He was distant. Somewhere else. I asked him several times what was wrong. He said it was nothing. He said he had a lot on his mind with work.

I would soon learn that "work" had a name and her name was Marisol. In that same visit he told me that they had hired a new on-air person. He said that he had been afraid to tell me about her for fear that I would be jealous. Jealous? I was never jealous just angry when you sleep with someone who isn't me. I mean sue me! He told me that she was a former Beauty Queen. His mom immediately looked her up. Of course she was pretty. Beauty pageants aren't for ugly girls right? Of course not. I started to realize that this was the reason he was so distant. He was putting his thoughts and energy into yet another bimbo. Yep, that's right, B-I-M-B-O. You have to be a pretty shady person to get involved with a married man with 2 kids? But the main person to blame was Ken.

Ken went back to Florida while the boys and I stayed in California for the remainder of our trip. I was a mess. I knew what was happening back in Florida. I had to keep it together for the boys and my family. Should we just stay in California? If he's cheating again why go back? The boys can just go to school here in California? For me, since I didn't have confirmation of an affair yet, we had to go back to Florida. We spent the remainder of the summer going to Disney World and getting the boys ready for school to start. Just when I thought I knew how bad it could get, I had no idea that really, the worst was yet to come.

The Lowest of the Low

While the boys and I had been in California my dad had started having trouble swallowing. It was at times, difficult for him to swallow food. Before we left he had made an appointment with an Ear, Nose and Throat doctor. The doctor had come to the conclusion that he simply had acid reflux. He prescribed him a muscle relaxer and acid reducer. It didn't help. He decided to get a second opinion and that appointment would take place after we went back to Florida.

    I will never forget the moment that changed everything. Ken, the boys and I were at Disney World. I knew my Daddy's appointment was that day and I was waiting to hear what had happened. I text my Mama. She wrote back saying that she would tell me everything when we got back home. I didn't like that. I wanted to know. I called her while we were waiting to go on a ride. She was mad at me for calling. She didn't want to ruin our time. It was bad. Doctors had done an endoscopy on my Daddy's esophagus. They found something and the doctors said it didn't look good. She still was holding on to hope that they couldn't be absolutely sure until the biopsy came back. I knew. I couldn't even say it. I cried so hard right there in Disney World. It was one of the worst days of my life.

Just a few days later it was confirmed that it was indeed cancer. My Mama had really convinced herself that it wasn't so it was very hard for her to take. I had already prepared myself and began doing what I do best. Research. Knowledge is power and I was gearing up as much as I could. There was no other way. My Daddy would beat this. My Mama wasn't taking it well at all. I knew I couldn't go to California since the boys were in school. I had to be with them both. My Daddy was very strong but my Mama was breaking and I couldn't stand to hear it. In talking with his co-anchor, Ken discovered that her best friend's mother had the very same diagnosis of esophageal cancer and she had survived. She was still alive and that diagnosis was 10 years ago! And what do you know, the doctor was practicing at a hospital in Florida! I knew I had to get my parents out here and my dad to THAT doctor. So I did.

Within a day or two, my parents were on a plane headed to Florida. We booked their return tickets for 6 weeks later. I didn't know what treatment would be like or how much time they would need to be in Florida but they were going to be exactly where they needed to be. With me. In that time my Mama and I were on the phone constantly. Changing insurance. Making appointments. It was a great distraction from the reality that my Daddy had cancer. Stage 3 Esophageal cancer.

My Daddy's first appointment was upon us and we took the 40-minute trek to the hospital. My Mama was much more calm now that she was with me. But once we encountered a problem with the switch in insurance, she almost lost it. We got around it and were able to see the doctor. After all of the research I had done I assumed the doctor would want to do surgery first then chemo and radiation second. That was not the case. After a very serious conversation with the doctor it would be decided that my Daddy would be getting hit with a full 24-hour dose of chemo on a weekly basis. He would spend the night in the hospital while the chemo was pumped through his body through a port that would be implanted in his chest. My Daddy was an amazing trooper. As he was being poked and prodded he would smile and be the reassuring voice to my Mama and me. Most of the time I would have to look the other way when they were doing anything to him that required needles. The nurses would look at me and say, "Girl, you better sit down."

It was an incredibly stressful time to say the least. My marriage was crumbling, again, and my Daddy had cancer. I wasn't eating at all. My clothes were starting to fall off of me. At my heaviest before all hell broke loose, I weighed 140 lbs. When I stepped on the scale after my parents arrived, the scale read 112 lbs. It wasn't healthy but there was nothing I could do. I remember that even as my Daddy couldn't eat he was still trying to take care of all of us. He made lasagna from scratch one night. It smelled amazing. I got it in front of me and I could barely take a bite. I felt so bad. My Daddy couldn't even enjoy it and would have loved to if his throat would allow him.

    The same week my Daddy started treatment I kicked Ken out of the house. It was September 11, 2011. I found an email that he had sent to the beauty queen and that did it for me. I called him into our bedroom and asked him to explain. He blamed me saying, "Why do you keep looking for things? You're crazy!" Really? I'm crazy? He then told me that he never loved me. I cried and he was mean. Same old story. It was the most frustrating thing in the world. I can't describe how it feels when you are trying to get through to someone and they just don't listen. How could he be so selfish? Wasn't I already going through enough with my Daddy being sick? I felt helpless and so incredibly sad.

    I sent Marisol an email asking her if she was having an affair with my husband. What was she gonna say? Yes? Only a gutsy woman would do that and that's not what I was dealing with here. She got back to me and said that wasn't how it was with them. Whatever honey. I wasn't born yesterday.

    I remember after he packed his bag and left, I went to take a shower. As I was in the shower I was just letting the water hit my skinny bruised body. I washed my hair and clumps of it came out. I got out of the shower and wrapped my hair in a towel. I sat down on the floor of the bathroom and just cried. I looked around me and saw that there was a trail of ants making their way to the cupboards under my sink. I cried some more. God spoke to me in that moment. I said out loud, "This is the lowest of the low, it will only get better from here." As if she could feel my pain, my Mama knocked on the door to check on me. I let her in and sobbed some more. I told her what I had told myself just minutes before. This was the lowest of the low. It would get better for all of us and we had that to look forward to. She agreed and we cried together. It would be the last time I would ever allow myself to feel that much pain in one day.

I woke up that next morning and realized I needed to see a therapist now! I got online and checked for doctors in my area. I saw a name that sounded American enough. Amazingly, I called that first one on the list and was in to see her just an hour later. God was working here, too. She was amazing and she was part of saving my life. I saw this therapist once a week.

I threw myself into the things that really mattered now. My Daddy, my Mama, and my boys. I held it together pretty well. My Mama and I took my Daddy to his appointments. I took my boys to school and even went to the gym. That helped a lot to feel a sense of normalcy. I started to embrace being alone. I lit candles, took baths, watched movies in my bedroom. All stuff I couldn't do when the king of the castle was living with us. All of our lives depended on his precious sleep. Yes, I know he gets up in the middle of the night to go to work but it doesn't have to be that hard! We are all doing our parts in this life! Take a nap and get over it.

My Daddy's treatment was taking a huge toll on his body. He was so constipated, had zero energy, and was getting huge sores on his lips. It was awful to see him this way.

During that same time he decided to have a talk with Ken. My mom and I had gone out shopping. Ken had said he was coming by to get some more things while we were gone. Instead of staying in the casita, my dad decided to wait for Ken in the main house. I didn't know this at the time. My Mama and I came home and saw Ken's car, still in the driveway. My stomach dropped. I knew my dad wasn't strong enough to hit Ken but what was going on. We walked in and the two of them were in deep conversation. Strangely enough, both of their faces lit up when I walked in. Immediately Ken grabbed me and said he needed to talk to me. We walked out and sat by the pool. He told me how he wanted to come home. That was the first thing he said. I just looked at him and said, "Are you sorry?" He said that he was but almost made me feel stupid for asking. I wanted to believe him so badly. All I ever wanted is for my family to be together. I told him that maybe when my parents go back to California he could come home. He seemed satisfied with that.

Looking back now I think he was happy to be able to act single for a little while longer but also knowing he would have a place to live again. It was never about coming back home to me or even the boys. It was about geography and keeping up the charade. I know that now.

My parents had made plans to head back to California and continue my Daddy's treatment there. My mom had missed 6 weeks of work and her company was being so amazing and understanding. My Daddy owned his own business so he was the only person he had to report to. My parents were extremely nervous to leave me and the boys. They had seen Ken for the person he truly was, again. My Daddy, was oddly optimistic. He had felt really good about the talk he'd had with Ken. He actually said that he wondered if maybe the reason he got cancer was to be able to come to Florida and have that important talk with Ken. I felt a lump in my throat. That is what a truly amazing man my Daddy is. I knew Ken would never ever listen. I hugged my parents, cried and said goodbye. It was the end of September 2011.

Who Am I

My therapist was amazing and to this day I know God put her in my life. No doubt. She was exactly what I needed. She knew about mental health and she was a Christian. She would use scripture in our sessions which allowed me to understand absolutely everything with eyes wide open. I talked about my relationship with Ken and his emotional and physical abuse, as if we were talking about the weather. You have to remember that it was my normal. I didn't know any different. When someone takes a hold of you and has complete control over you, you don't know any different.

    She really wanted Ken to come in for a joint session with us. I asked him and he reluctantly agreed. That day he met me at her office after work. I spoke a little and then he spoke. He had a very laid back matter-of-fact attitude with her. She calmly asked him questions and he calmly answered. She asked him how he felt about the marriage. He told her, "I could go on like this forever." "What do you mean by that?" She asked. "The way things are now, I'm fine with it." Ken said. At our next session alone my therapist very frankly asked me, "Is that how he always is?" I told her yes. I will never forget how she said it. "Oh sweetheart, you know that's not ok, right?" I didn't. Like I said, it was my normal. I was so numb and used to the emotional abuse. She then preceded to tell me that he would most likely never change. He was a classic narcissist. Possibly a sociopath. Only with intense therapy and his willingness to get better would he ever have a chance of changing. But he was fine with who he was, fine with the marriage the way it was, and for those reasons, there was no chance of change.

It was up to me to now decide what to do. She gave me the scenario that he was this runaway truck and I was holding on to this frayed rope that was attached to the truck. The truck was dragging me all over the road. My body was getting skinned and scraped with every sharp turn and bump that truck made. All I had to do was let go of the truck and I would be alright. The bumps and bruises I had gotten from the truck would eventually heal. I just had to do it. I had to let go. It was the most amazing realization I had ever had. No one could have explained it better.

I describe the next several months as living in a dream world. Not a good dream and not a nightmare. Just sort of floating above myself and powering through everyday. I know that God kept me going. God and my beautiful boys. I felt strength that had to be from Him.

I prayed all the time. He was absolutely with me. I found a church nearby and the boys and I would go. I had invited Ken to go with us, but he had no interest.

Ken had moved back in and we were going through the motions. Christmas time came and things felt ok. He was on his best behavior. He asked me for a list of everything I wanted that year and he got just about everything on it. I needed to take back the tennis bracelet he had bought me because it was too big so I asked him for the receipt. I guess he had forgotten about the other purchases he had made because there was a necklace on that receipt that was unaccounted for. I ended up asking about it and he of course came up with something saying he had bought it for me but had returned it because he realized he had gotten me plenty. Hmmm? Ok? I knew it was a lie but I let it go. Just days later a very prominent necklace showed up on the neck of the beauty queen in one of her Twitter pictures.

I had stopped bringing any of these discoveries to his attention. It's just amazing what you find out when you're not even looking. It was pointless and he would always say I was crazy. More shots to my heart and more of the silent dying inside.

I had the most low night of my life shortly after this. After an afternoon of drinking with him, I saw her name come up on his phone as she texted. It sent me over the edge. The boys were in bed and I was feeling so low and worthless. I blame it on the alcohol. The alcohol and my horrible husband. I just wanted the pain to end. I told him I wanted to die. I went into the bathroom and laid out every Xanax I had. I think there were about 14. I told him that I was gonna take them all and whatever else I could find. He didn't care. Instead of helping me through he took video of me on my lowest day. I ended up taking 4 Xanax. I felt so sad. I went to bed. He never checked on me and didn't care. No surprise. I would never let anyone have that much power over me ever again. Ever.

In my mind I had begun to think about leaving him for good. How could I take the boys 3000 miles away from their father? Why were we brought to Florida if we were just going to go back to California separated again? All of these answers would be revealed in time.

When your husband cheats I think most women want to know everything. We all do our research and become the best investigators. For some reason we think it's going to make us feel better knowing every single detail. I think it's our brains distracting us from our hearts. The need for more information keeps our hearts from breaking right there on the spot. But one day, you just stop looking. Your heart and mind can no longer take anymore info. Enough is enough. How much proof do you need? Your husband is a total scumbag.

    I stopped looking for clues to his affair. It was pointless. In this case it was absolutely undeniable. Once a cheater. Always a cheater. I wasn't looking the other way I just knew that I really was stuck there for now and the best thing for me was to go on without more confirmation. God wanted to make sure I knew what he was up to. He was constantly throwing things in my face. I would be hanging up Ken's pants and a receipt would fall from the pocket. A receipt from a place and a time when he said he was somewhere else. I went online to pay a parking ticket for him, at his request, and there was a new parking ticket at a place and time when he shouldn't have been there. It was a slap in the face every time. I knew what I was being told. "It's time to go."

    It was January 2012 and I kicked him out again. He would call me or text me in the middle of the night to say that he didn't have a place to stay. I didn't care. Stay with her. To which he would respond, "Who?" Really? He would say he was sleeping in his car and I would say, "Good." Good night. I was really disconnecting. I was starting to become numb to him. He had been so Jekyll and Hyde our whole marriage. I was over it. I didn't want any part of it anymore. I was actually starting to let go. I began to keep my head down and get through these next few months. But he loved the drama.

An Actress In Her Best Role

Ken's dad had made plans to come out for a golf tournament and coincidentally Ken convinced me that he should come back home. So he moved back in. It was Super Bowl Sunday February 2012. Ken and I both began to drink a lot more when he was around. Our favorite at that time was a John Daly. It's an Arnold Palmer mixed with vodka. For me it was the only way I could be around him. I guess I can probably say the same for him. We had to of course, play nice for his Dad. That night we had gone to bed and we were watching TV. He was angry, again, probably because he lost his bets for the day (as usual). I remember it like it was yesterday. He asked me to give him the remote so I tossed it to him. He thought I threw it to him too hard so he turned around in bed and backhanded me with it. I was in shock. He had shaken me many times before. He had grabbed me and thrown me and even the occasional slap here and there. This time he hit me so hard in the face. It was so hard that the impact made me see stars. I felt my lip swelling by the second. I started to cry because of the pain and also the craziness that had just happened. This was getting scary. My tooth was stuck in my lip and the minute I moved it with my tongue the blood began to flow. I couldn't believe what had just happened. I didn't call the police. I should have. So many times. He was out of control and getting worse. I went into the bathroom. I had enough sense to take a picture of my face and lip. I sent it to my best friend Taylor telling her to hang on to it just in case. I was starting to fear him even more. He knew he was losing control of me and he didn't like it. What would happen next? I cleaned myself up and as crazy as it sounds, I crawled back in to our bed. I cried myself to sleep. Ken never asked me if I was ok.

The next day I woke up and the injury on my lip was as clear as day. I couldn't hide it. I made up a story to tell. I dropped the soap in the shower and hit my lip on the faucet. Brilliant. Same story for everyone. They all seemed satisfied. Nobody asked any questions. Even Ken's dad. That really angers me now. I was talking to my best friend just about every day. She was so worried. She wanted me to leave immediately. I told her I knew what I was doing. I really didn't but I was good at faking it.

My parents knew nothing. I stayed strong and didn't want to burden them with more than was already on their full plate. My Daddy was ending his months of treatment of chemo and radiation. He had been through hell. He had lost over 40lbs. His body was so weak that just a walk to the kitchen would warrant a nap. They would find out the extent of things in time. Just not now.

Being Ken's wife still meant I had to keep the charade going. I was learning that this marriage was a business to Ken. He knew that he had to keep me and the boys around to look like the perfect guy. It came time for an annual work party. It was at a beautiful famous hotel. It was a party for all of the big media buyers. The talent had to schmooze the buyers and spouses were invited in on the fun. I bought a dress specifically for that night. He never took me out anywhere. I knew once again, that this was all apart of the game. I didn't care and I was just looking forward to going out and having a good time. The station sent a town car to take us to the hotel. Ken's dad was there so he was happy to watch the boys. The boys were even excited to see the both of us dressed up and going out together.

On the way there we had wine and picked up his co-anchor and her husband. They were a great couple and it was nice to have someone else with us. I remember he wanted to take a picture of us and post it on Facebook. I was a little shocked but I went with it. For one night, I felt special even if it really was all about him.

We started out at a steakhouse inside the hotel. We ordered so much food and the drinks were flowing. It felt good to be out with adults and to be reaping some of the benefits of this hard job of mine as Ken's wife. He barely talked to me or noticed me. Typical. I was good at fending for myself and I was used to it. I was just trying to have a good time. I kept myself busy that night drinking vodka, wine and whatever anyone handed me.

I watched as Ken was a pro at being a whore. It was a trait I used to be proud of since he was so good at talking to people and getting them to trust him and like him immediately. But now, it was just disgusting. I wondered if any of these women had been in bed with my husband. I now know that yes they had. Looking back on that night I realized that I had been handed off to someone in the sales department as sort of a, "Here, watch her and make sure she doesn't get in the way." I never got in the way. I was always the supportive wife. The stupid, clueless, supportive wife.

The party moved on to one of the clubs inside the hotel. I'm a dancer remember and I absolutely love to dance. So that's what I did. Some of the sales people and a few of the female anchors and I were dancing. We were having a great time laughing and letting loose. All of a sudden I felt a hard squeeze on my arm and I was being yanked off of the dance floor. It was Ken and he was mad as hell and I didn't know why. He took me to a corner of the club and started screaming at me. He was saying, "Why are you acting like such a whore?" What? "What are you talking about?" I asked. He said he saw me dancing dirty with one of the sales guys and it was totally embarrassing. Are you serious? I said, "Do you mean Quincy? Quincy's gay you know?" Of course he knew that Quincy's gay. He was one of Ken's good friends. Just then Quincy came over with a nervous look on his face. He consoled Ken like the little baby he was, swooped him up, and just like that, there I was alone in the corner.

    I wandered back to the tables and sat down. The waitress was there within seconds so I ordered another drink. Everyone was looking at me like I had done something terrible. What was wrong with these people? Ken was the star and if he wasn't happy, then nobody was. Had I done something wrong? He always made me question myself. Was I crazy? Nope. That was Ken. I sat there and drank my drink when I was scooped up and told it was time to go. My arm was aching by the time we reached the lobby. Ken was squeezing it so tight. I felt like a little girl who was being punished by her father. But no, my father would never, ever treat me this way. The car was waiting and the driver greeted me with a smile. Oh finally a friendly face. Ken pushed me in to the back seat and we were off.

    The whole way home he screamed at me. At first I tried to defend myself. He was saying, "It was so embarrassing to see you dancing like that. What were you thinking?" I didn't understand one bit. I asked him, "What was I doing?" He said, "You were looking sexy and all of the guys were loving it." Oh, so that's what this was about. I was actually looking sexy and for some reason that made him uncomfortable. There was just no getting through to him. There never was. It was pointless. Every time I did try to say anything he would just get angrier and angrier so I just stopped talking. We were getting closer to home and Ken told the driver to drive through McDonald's. Ken ordered and they handed him the food. He didn't ask me if I wanted anything. I asked him if I could have a chicken nugget and somehow that even enraged him. He grabbed a chicken nugget out of the box, looked at me with an evil look on his face and said, "You want this chicken nugget?" I said, "Yes, please." He dove over to my side of the car and smashed the hot chicken nugget against my face pushing it into my skin till it was all over me and the car. I was crying and couldn't believe how out of control he was.

I was in complete shock and wanted out of that car. The driver looked in his rearview mirror in horror and all he could do was drive. We got out onto the main road towards our house and I tried the handle to get out. It was locked. I yelled to the driver, "Please unlock my door!" The car came to a screeching halt and he unlocked the door for me. I jumped out as fast as I could and took off. I left my shoes and my purse. I didn't care. I didn't know what he would do next. I ran on the side of the road, bare feet in my pretty dress. Tears were streaming down my face. I was sobbing and talking to myself out loud. "You gotta get outta here. You're gonna die. He's going to kill you!" What could I do? Where could I go? My precious boys deserved better. Why God? Please help me. I just kept running. I could feel the mud from the grass getting all over my legs and my dress. The only other thing I could feel was the sting of the burn on my cheek. Just then I heard a car pull up behind me. I turned around to see the town car. The headlights were blinding.

I kept running. The driver pulled along side me, put his window down and said, "Miss, please get in the car. It isn't safe." I stopped to look at him. He was a complete stranger but at that moment, I felt safer with him than I did with Ken. I reluctantly slid in the passenger seat. While I was getting in I glanced in the back seat and Ken was looking out the other window. What had gone on in the car while I was gone? I would never know. No other words were spoken by anyone on the rest of that drive home. We pulled up to our home. I opened my door, looked at the driver and gave him a half smile, almost to say thank you. He closed his eyes, nodded his head and he was off. I looked at Ken as we started walking into the foyer. He looked back at me with a mixture of hate and disappointment.

    The boys were asleep and so was Ken's dad. Thank God I didn't have to put on a show. I don't know how I would have. I walked into our bathroom and locked the door behind me. I stripped off that muddy dress, started the bath and got in the tub. I laid in the tub and let the water fill up to my chin. I wished I could just sleep here. I was scared now. All I could think about was protecting the boys. I couldn't let them see him like I just did. I had to protect their sweet innocent hearts. I cried and prayed. After my fingers and toes were wrinkled from being in the water so long I got out of the tub and put on my most comfy pajamas. I unlocked the door to find Ken snoring, still in his clothes on top of our bed. I tiptoed to my side of the bed, undid the covers and slid quietly into the bed. I was exhausted. Hopefully the morning would bring another, but much better day.

Big Decisions

The boys and I came to California for spring break 2012. I was so happy to be in California with my family and friends that loved me so much. I felt it and I knew what I had to do. Ken could feel it, too. He called more than usual while we were gone. I told him I wanted to stay. I told him I would enroll the boys in school in California. I didn't want to come back to Florida. There was nothing there for me or for the boys. He of course, convinced me to come back to Florida and I did.

Something about that trip to California changed me. I knew that I had to leave I just didn't know how or when. I had coffee with a friend who I had become so close to in Florida. I told her everything. Being so close, she basically knew. I was hiding it well to others but she knew me and I wasn't fooling her.

I began to make plans for the biggest move of my life. I was finally going to leave him, for good. I remember sitting in my beautiful home in Florida looking at all of the pictures I had so carefully placed on the walls, the curtains I had picked out, my great grandmother's chair I was sitting in. It would all have to be packed and shipped back to California.

What a process. But, I had to start somewhere. That day I picked up some boxes and some purple packing tape. If I was going to do this I was going to do it right and my way. I packed up my first box that day. My grandmother's crystal would be the first thing I would ship back to my parent's house in California.

    I was a mess inside but had to keep my head on straight and be a strong Mama for my boys. It was the hardest decision I would ever have to make. I was taking the boys 3,000 miles away from their father. Would they ever forgive me? Did they want to go? Was this the right thing? On our drives to school I would poke around asking the boys little questions here and there. One day I asked, "If we move back to California, we won't see Daddy very much. What do you think of that?" My oldest son responded, "We don't see him very much anyway." It broke my heart to hear that but it was true. Out of the mouths of babes. It gave me more of that confirmation I needed. I was making the right decision. I guess I wanted to be absolutely sure that I had done everything I could to make this marriage work. I had. I had done more than should ever be expected of me. It was ok to give up.

Ken wasn't around much at all. He would sometimes come home during the week and sometimes not. If he did come home it would be to sleep but not to interact with any of us. I really had no idea where he was spending his time. He would tell me that he was golfing or had a shoot for work but he wasn't around and I didn't really mind. There was a peace not having him home. There was no tension and no questions. I didn't care anymore and I was ok with the quiet. I started embracing being alone. The boys and I would enjoy the nights together and after they went to bed, it was "me" time. I would light candles in my room, draw a bath and turn on a movie. I had two favorite movies during that time. Eat, Pray, Love and Date Night. For some reason they brought me comfort. I have no idea why.

I prayed constantly. I was a wreck wondering if I was doing the right thing. The boxes were being packed and plans were being made. Ken didn't say a whole lot. I don't think he believed I would ever really leave. I guess I never believed I would either. Still, even after everything he had done to me and to this family, I wasn't sure if I was making the biggest mistake I have ever made. One morning it all seemed to be clear. I woke up with the lyrics to two different songs in my head. I had not heard either one of those songs in years, but I looked up the lyrics and it was clear what was being said. Get Here by Oleta Adams had always been a favorite song of my dad's…"I don't care how you get here, just get here if you can." Let Your Soul Be Your Pilot by Sting also spoke to me..."Let your soul guide you, he'll guide you well." It was all telling me what I needed to do. What I was already planning to do. I would get home to California and I was making the right choices. That day I would stop wondering and start planning the rest of my life.

Just 2 weeks before the boys and I were set to get on that plane back to California Ken was now being bold with his affair and loved throwing it in my face because I was leaving. He told me that he had promised "her" that he would go to a wedding with her. It was one of our last weekends in Florida and he was choosing to spend it with her. I begged him to spend it with his boys. I would go somewhere so he could just be at home alone with them. He didn't care. He was leaving and that was it. The boys were wondering where Daddy was going. He lied and told them he had to go in to work. I hated that he lied to them. I would vow to never lie to them. He promised that he would take them to Dave and Buster's tomorrow to make it up to them. He left. I opened a bottle of wine, made dinner for me and the boys and we watched a movie together, just the 3 of us. I was getting used to it being that way.

    The next day Ken didn't text or call for hours and hours. The boys kept asking me, "Where's Daddy? When's he gonna take us to Dave and Buster's?" I was calling and texting but couldn't get an answer from Ken. The boys were even texting and he wouldn't answer them. I finally just told them that I didn't know where Daddy was and I had no idea when he was coming home. I called my girlfriend and we decided to pack up the kids and head to the beach.
    I knew that once he finally decided to get around to the boys he would be furious at me for taking them to the beach. He wanted to do things at his time and pace and we were all supposed to just fall in line. Sorry, not this time. I wasn't sitting around another second waiting for him. We had a blast that day. The kids were happy to be out of the house playing and eating ice cream on the beach. It was a nice day until he decided to text around 3pm. It was a Sunday. The boys had school the next day. What was he thinking? He wasn't and he never did. He flipped out on me via text.

    I had reached my end in dealing with him. I called my parents crying. I didn't know what else to do. My mom just wanted me to get on a plane right then and there but it was so important to me for the kids to finish school. My mom said she would call Ken's step mom to make them aware of how terrible he was being. I don't think anything came from it but I was glad his family knew a little more whether they really cared or not. I was so scared to come home that day. I text him and told him that. I told him I didn't want for him to cause any scene in front of the boys. They were smart and we had just a couple more weeks of this place and we were out. When we got home he was oddly calm and nice. Maybe his dad had talked to him? I felt relief. Another day down.

Say Goodbye

That next week I reached out to his boss' wife. She and I had become very close and I knew I could trust her even with what I was about to tell her. I sent her a message talking about how I was truly worried about Ken. He was spinning out of control and I feared that he would downward spiral without me or the boys here to try and ground him. I told her that I had hoped she and her husband would really watch over Ken as they had become sort of adopted parents to us. They loved us. They loved our boys. We were lucky to have them in our lives. Ken was lucky that his boss had given him this chance of a job after everything else. I was worried that Ken would blow yet another job. It was all he would have left when we would leave. I told her that one of the big reasons we were leaving was because of the beauty queen they had hired (and fired since she sucked). She had been the final straw that broke this marriage. I had hoped that we could have lunch before we left town. I also told her that I was telling her this in confidence. Ken would be furious if he knew what I was telling her. He wanted to keep all of his secrets to keep up that perfect persona he had so carefully constructed.

Just a few hours later I saw my life flash before my eyes. Not only did the boss' wife not keep what I told her a secret but she told her husband who then called to talk to Ken about it! He came at me after that conversation like I had never seen before in my life. He cornered me in the living room against the wall. He put his hand on my throat and said, "I could kill you right now." I looked at him in the eyes and said, "Please don't do this in front of the boys." At that moment my oldest son walked in and said, "Daddy, what are you doing to Mama?" He took his hand off of me and the rage subsided. I told my son that Daddy was just playing. Ken continued to yell at me throughout that day and night. The boys kept asking me why was Daddy so mad and I just shook it off saying he was tired. I will never miss those moments of fear and rage. They changed me. He had changed me forever.

Time was ticking by. I felt stronger and stronger with every bag I packed and box I taped. It was so easy to decide what I would take and what I would leave. I remember going through the drawers and cupboards in the kitchen. I took the coffee mugs. But I left the dishes. He could eat off of the plates we got from our wedding. I took out all of the pictures from their frames to save myself any pain when I unpacked them again. I didn't want any reminders of what had been. I only wanted to look forward. I had no idea when I would ever be able to unpack in my new home but it would happen. It would someday. Arrangements were made. We would be on a plane the very day the boys got out of school. The movers would pick up my things that same day. So much to do but I was really doing it. I was leaving.

The boys were so excited to go back to California. They never really liked their school in Florida and for some reason to them, it never felt much like home. They later referred to that school as "the school that must not be named." That was all them. I had nothing to do with that. Maybe they were picking up on my vibe? Maybe I wasn't hiding everything as good as I thought. My boys were smart and they wanted their Mama to be happy, too.

I had thought of everything. Boxes were packed, flights were booked and even my little mini doxie was taking the flight home with us once again. It was a lot to handle but I was ready and God was with me through every step of the way. Ken came home from work that morning early so he could be with me. Why? I have no idea. I guess it may have finally hit him in a way. We were all leaving and would not be coming back. He called to ask me if I wanted anything to eat and all that sounded good on that hot June day in Florida was a big iced cold Coke. He brought me one. We talked a little small talk as he looked around the house at all of the boxes and suitcases. He held me and started to cry. He asked me not to go. He did say that he was sorry. It felt strange to see this kind of emotion from him. The last time I remember seeing this was after his first affair and he begged me not to leave him then. I cried and of course I felt sad but my mind had finally been made up and there was no changing it. Ken picked up the boys from school that last day as I finished up some last packing and got ready for the flight.

That ride to the airport Ken didn't know what to do. He started playing with his water bottle that same way he had done before. Another bad memory. The boys and I were just so excited and he was in a completely different place. He hugged us all as he dropped us at the curb. To this day I look back and I wonder how the hell could he have let us all go? It's unbelievable to me. I could never allow my family to leave me. But I was nothing like him. We said our goodbyes. It was very easy for the boys and me.

This time it would be for good. From that moment on we would be living full-time in California without him. I didn't feel one bit sad. Not for me or the boys. We were all better off being far away from him. He was a fair-weather father. The novelty of having his family around would always wear off. We deserved better.

Looking back I can't remember a time that I really felt remorse from him. I think it was more anger for getting caught. The blame somehow kept being put on me. And I somehow believed him. I was caught in this crazy web of lies and I was living the biggest one of all. How could I ever believe our marriage could ever go back to good again? I should have INSISTED on counseling, church, more family time. I know that these were all pieces of the foundation of a marriage that I wanted. He just wanted to sweep it all under the rug. A rug that could no longer cover the lies, hurt and pain. I would tell him that I was in so much pain and couldn't shake this hopeless feeling. He wouldn't comfort me. All he would say is "I'm sorry. It won't happen again." No hugs. No eye contact. No feeling. I realized that it had nothing to do with the woman I wasn't, but everything to do with the man that he was.

When we got checked in for our flight I sat down and wrote an email to Ken. He had been texting me since he dropped us off. He was saying things like he was dying inside and why did we have to go. Why? Did you forget what you did to me and to these boys all these years?

This is the email...

So as I sit in the airport waiting to board our flight back home to Cali, I find myself full of things that I need to say to you. I don't know why I bother because after all of these years and tears it never seems to get through to you, but here goes. Consider this my last and final words to you.
I am so incredibly sad. Everywhere I go all over this darn country I am reminded by memories of you. Memories of us and memories of what once was, our beautiful family. For some reason you do not see me as important to you in your life. For some reason you never want to listen to me or hear me. I have loved you from the day that I met you. Yes we married young and had the usual ups and downs of a relationship but I did nothing to make you treat me the way that you have. I know what I did wrong. I stayed. I should have left you all those years ago when I found out that I was pregnant with our second child and then the very next day had your affair with your co-anchor confirmed. Maybe you would have changed? Maybe not. I will never know.

I did what I thought was right for me and the family and I stayed. I gave it another chance. I loved you that much and I believed in you that you would do the right thing but you didn't. I trusted you again and the weekend of my baby shower you had sex with a stranger. That should have been it. But again I stayed. It goes on and on. I loved you too much and you took advantage of me over and over again. All I wanted was a husband and father to lead our family. I kept believing in you and your potential and you just got worse and worse. That is my fault for just being a doormat and taking it every single time. It should be no surprise to me that we are over but there is still so much sadness and anger for the choices you continue to make. You stopped respecting me for letting you just live your single life as a married man. I was just trying to make you happy anyway I could even if that meant losing myself.

After the stalking stuff and my support for you through all of that I thought my prayers were finally answered. You wanted to renew your vows with me and boy did you mean it. I saw the look in your eyes on that day and felt your love and devotion. All of my dreams were coming true. You were a good man, a good husband and a good father. All I could have ever wanted. It felt amazing. We talked about our hopes and dreams. We held each other when we had bad days. We cried. We laughed. It was a true marriage and it felt wonderful. There was no getting out. We were sticking it out together forever. The four of us. Our life of ups and downs was taking us up again to a new life in Florida. It was amazing and exciting and God was blessing our beautiful family. Life was going great and we had it all. We really did have it all. I know you hate hearing that but it's the truth. You got bored with your everyday life again and had to look outside of our marriage again. It's just awful. You blame me but it's you. Life was so good and you ruined it. I will never understand why. I will never forget but someday I will forgive. The hurt is too fresh right now to even think about forgiving. You continue to hurt me by the way you talk to me. By the things you say to the boys in front of me and to them. I saw a little of what you said to her about me and I can only imagine the lies you have told and the lies you have convinced yourself of. It's all so embarrassing and disgraceful. I know that you love your new life in Florida with your new girl because she just thinks you are wonderful. And at a time you were wonderful. You are handsome, a talented drummer and news anchor. Your career ahead of you is amazing. I am sad I don't get to be apart of it since it

became my dream for you and for us. But don't forget that I was the woman who loved you. I supported you when you had nothing. I gave you two beautiful boys. I gave you confidence every day even when you were screwing around. I made you healthy lunches and healthy dinners. I provided a good home. I did your laundry. And I did it all because I loved you and I loved our family. What did I get in return? Nothing. Absolutely nothing.
I know God has an amazing plan for me. I know the man of my dreams is out there. The hurt will hopefully go away sooner than later. Soon I will have to sit the boys down to tell them that Daddy and Mama are getting divorced. When they ask me why I will come up with something that protects their little hearts because that is the right thing to do and I am a damn good mother. It's my most prized quality. I will always put them first. And when my new husband comes around, me and the boys will be his first priority because that it what is right and what a good man does.
I will always be sad that it didn't work out for you and me. I will always be sad that these boys don't get to have their mother and their father together just as God intended. I will have no regrets though. I did everything and then some to keep this family together. The reality is that

you love your single life more than anything. I wish I had known this years ago but life goes on and I will go on, too. I pray for peace, happiness and love for myself and these boys. I pray that you live the life you are meant to and when you are around your boys you be the best example of a man you can possibly be. I realize that as a single mom I have so much to teach them. I will because it's my job.
I hope you pray and that God touches your heart with all the things that He wants for you and you listen to Him even if it's not at all what you want. This is my goodbye to you.

    He responded to me with something that really had nothing to do with all I had wrote. I had poured out my heart and again and again he never listened. He never cared. I was really done. That would be the last email or message that I would send him about us. The hurt was so fresh but it would only get better from here. I couldn't wait to get home and get strong again. I needed those people who would pull me back up again. I am forever grateful to my family and friends who were there for me.

    Every part of that day was a step by step process. Each piece of that day put the final puzzle picture together. The last step for me was getting on that plane. I remember immediately feeling a sense of relief. The boys and I were in our seats and our little doggy was comfortably tucked below my feet. Our little family was together. Nothing would ever break that up. I took a deep breath, closed my eyes to fight off the tears, and then smiled. I had done it. Finally we were leaving. It felt so good.

My parents picked us up at LAX that night. They hid it pretty well but they were both wrecks. They wanted us all home. Things had gotten so bad. All they wanted to do was hug us. That's all I wanted, too. I hadn't felt a good hug in so long. Since they last visited. I hugged both my mom and dad so tight. My mom got tears in her eyes and so did I. The worst part of this nightmare was over. The boys were so happy. I told my parents I would probably sleep for a week since I had not slept solidly in months.

That first night I slept so great. My dad had pressed the sheets and turned down the bed in anticipation of our arrival. He wanted us to always feel loved and cared for. It was such a nice but unfamiliar feeling. Something I had forgotten. We all got up that next morning so happy to be back in California with our loving family. It was priceless.

My parents would be celebrating their 40th wedding anniversary that weekend with a big party of family and friends. It was the perfect welcome back. Everyone kept telling me how great I looked. They said I had a glow about me. I guess it was freedom. I got a couple of family friends asking if I was really alright. I did just make a huge life decision. I told them all I felt great and I was looking forward to the future. I really did and I really was.

I stayed busy that first month back. I made play date plans for the boys and I reconnected with friends. To a few of my friends I felt that I owed them an apology. I had abandoned them and abandoned our friendship I told them that I would never lose sight of the important things in life. The important people. I was changing me and I was trying to find that girl I used to be. Surrounding myself with those that really loved me made that part easy. I was coming back. I was laughing again. I started to realize that I couldn't remember the last time that I had cried. I used to cry just about every day. No more of that. I was moving onward and upward. It felt so good. I even started feeling the confidence to dress like a girl again. I know that sounds strange but I had gotten so lost in him that I had sort of forgotten that I was a woman! I had so much black and brown in my wardrobe it was sad. I had a bunch of big t-shirts and pants that covered my body. I started wearing brighter colors and more form-fitting clothes and began to look like the woman that I was!

In that same time I had connected with the beauty queen's ex-boyfriend. Yep that's right. He had actually contacted me almost a year before telling me about the affair through Facebook Messenger. However, since we weren't friends the message went to another "other" folder which I didn't even know existed. I didn't see the message until about 4 months later when I was very aware of the affair. We began a very interesting relationship via Facebook. We were rooting for each other in life. I remember telling him that he had dodged a bullet with the beauty queen and he came back saying that he had dodged a nuclear bomb!

When July rolled around things really started to sink in. I felt this sort of "what's next?" feeling. What would be next? What would I do now? It was time to face reality. The boys and I both felt it. We clung to each other and started to move forward. We made plans and got excited about our future together. The rest of July ticked by and then came August 2012. This month was the beginning of my single life.

New Chapters

It was at this time that I was ready to finalize my divorce. I had filed back in 2008. I had not filed the final papers so the divorce was ruled a default. In 2008, I had not asked for alimony and the child support was very low since Jason wasn't making nearly as much as he was now. The case was still open so I filed papers to amend the child support, custody and add alimony. The clerk at the court said as long as we came up with a parenting plan on our own to work out all of the custody arrangements, the judge would sign off and we would be good to go. There was a court date calendared for October but I was sure we wouldn't need it. That would become one of the biggest wrong assumptions of my life!

I had been borrowing my mom's car since we had moved back from Florida. My car remained in Florida. I was trying to figure out the best way possible to get it and came to the conclusion that I needed to fly there and drive it back to California. I made the plans and flew my best friend Taylor out to drive back with me. I was so busy planning out the boys schedule for that week I would be gone that I didn't even give much thought to how amazing this trip was going to be.

I flew out to Florida first and Ken picked me up at the airport. It was strange seeing him. I was tired from the red eye flight but so excited for the trip I had ahead. It was a little emotional for me. I think being tired added to it for sure. I brought a copy of the parenting plan I had come up with and had been trying to get him to sign. He quickly looked it over and signed it. It was mid August 2012. That would become very important. We sat in my car. I cried and wished him well. As I drove off from his station parking lot I had so many emotions going through my mind and body. I was happy to have more freedom now having my car, I was looking forward to the trip ahead and I was sad to end this chapter of my life. I cried hard for that first part of the drive. I called my Mama and my best friends to tell them I had gotten the hard part over with. They were all so worried how he was going to act towards me. Luckily I had gotten him on a pretty good day. God was with me.

I met up with some friends in Florida. They knew the stress I had been through so they were excited to take me out and help me to forget it all! The next day Taylor would fly in and we were almost ready for our cross country journey! Our plan was to drive from Florida to Mobile, AL that first day. Taylor and I talked the entire time of that first trip. We took stops and were sure to take video of everything. I had planned on editing some kind of video diary for our friends and family. Funny thing was, Ken was so interested in where we were and what we were up to. It was weird. Taylor found it more annoying than anything. I was still trying to appease him in some strange way. All I know is after this summer, my eyes were wide open. I was single and on the prowl for sure. Things had changed in me. It was a different feeling but I liked it and I didn't want it to end any time soon. We made it AL to stay at Taylor's friend's house. She had met him on her music festival tours. We would stay at his family's home. We had sushi and laughed our butts off! It was so sweet and nice. We were comfortable.

    The next morning bright and early we were headed to our next stop. Austin, TX. We were most excited about Austin. It was the one place we knew we were gonna go out and have a good time. We were both single and ready to meet some cowboys. We finally made it to Austin. We were tired but no way was that going to keep us from having a blast in this city, together. We immediately went to the hotel bar and ordered a drink. It was just what we needed to get us going. We went back up to the room to get ready for a night on the town. We would be in Austin one night and headed back out on the road in the morning. We had the music turned up loud, another drink from the hotel bar, and the curling irons were hot. Finally, we were ready. Let's do this!

Our night out in Austin proved to be a success based on the size of our hangovers! We headed to a dive bar for some greasy burgers and fries. It helped but we were tired and knew we couldn't make the entire way to what was supposed to be our next stop, Albuquerque, NM. So we decided to make a little pit stop in Dallas. It was a little out of the way but Taylor had another music friend there so a little detour to Dallas it was! We woke up the next morning to our alarm but we were feeling good and ready to make it to our next destination. Let's try this again, Albuquerque, NM.

The scenery was beyond beautiful. We sure have a gorgeous country. I highly recommend a road trip to take it all in. I guess it was pretty awesome to do it at such an important time of my life and with my best friend. Absolutely amazing. We made our way to Albuquerque. For some reason that stop was so nice. The hotel we chose was so comfortable and we had our own big beds that we could spread out in. We changed and decided to grab some good Mexican food and a margarita. We deserved it! That detour to Dallas cost us some big time so we had a long day. After dinner we got comfy in our big cozy beds, watched a little Beverly Hills 90210 reruns and fell asleep.

The next morning was a little bittersweet. It would be the last day of our journey across the country. I missed my boys terribly. I had of course talked to them many times on the trip. They were a little out of sorts and they needed their Mama back. Before I left, I had prepared a schedule for the boys for the entire time I was gone. I wanted them to stay busy since I knew they would miss me. This was the longest we had ever gone not seeing each other. I kept telling them how great it would be to have our own car back. We would have more freedom to do whatever we wanted. Just the 3 of us.

Taylor and I had such a blast. We didn't fight once! Then again, we never fought. We laughed! We danced! It was hilarious. She's my best friend and I love her dearly.

We got in to LA around 9pm on a Friday night. We made it! It was such an amazing trip and we had made it safely. I turned around and headed back to my parent's house. I was exhausted but I couldn't wait to see my boys!

When I turned the corner I could see them sitting on the driveway waiting for me! They had the biggest smiles on their faces. It brought tears to my eyes. We now had our car and a little more independence and that was exciting for all of us.

The Grind

That next week the boys started school at their new school (again) near my parent's house. It was going to be so great for them to start making new friends and moving on from our life in Florida. We'd had an awesome summer but now it was time to get down to business and daily life.

While they were in school I started writing my book and looking for jobs. I was worried about Ken paying me. He would pay me here and there. I guess when he was in a good mood and got paid it would show up in our joint account. I would take it out immediately so he wouldn't change his mind. He was completely in charge of our finances still and there was no support order in effect, yet. I was helpless and had no access to any money. My parents were amazing. My Daddy wasn't working anymore due to the cancer and my Mama had a decent paying job as a paralegal. They took us in and paid for everything for me and the boys. I did what I could for them. I cleaned their house and when I would get any money from Ken I would buy groceries and pitch in as much as I possibly could.

I was looking for jobs constantly. It was just so important that I be there for the boys before and after school. I know that they needed that stability and my parents were so supportive of that. They knew that I was a good Mama.

I was determined to not let this situation change much for them. I took them to school always telling them to find the beauty in every day. I picked them up with chocolate milk and a snack asking them how their day went. We always did homework right after school. I wanted them to always be in the habit of getting it done. They were and have always been my priority. I never wanted them to look back and say I didn't do everything I could for them. That first week of school went great for them. They were happy and settling in to life in California beautifully.

The next weekend Taylor and I headed to the airport to go to Canada to see some friends. She paid for my ticket. She said I could pay her back someday. We took more video and laughed the whole time. We flew in to Saskatoon, Saskatchewan. It was another adventure with my best friend! I was getting my confidence back. I was coming back to that girl I used to be. Goodbye Canada. What a blast. Time for more adventures!

We got in to San Diego on Labor Day 2012. We were so tired but what a great time. It took a week or so to get back into the swing of life again. I started working out and getting into shape. I had lost all of that weight but I needed some serious toning. At the gym I ran into and old friend. He was a guy that was a few years older than me. He was a trainer at the gym and he was hot! We will call him Dash. He wanted to train me for free! OK, don't be naive! It started out as training but quickly turned into dating. A lesson to myself now would be to never date trainers and to also not think every guy you date is going to be the one!

I had a lot to learn about dating. I never really got the experience but for a couple little boyfriends in high school. I was committed to Ken when I was 17! My quick relationship with Dash got my feet wet and my heart hurt a little but I was on my way to finding what I really wanted now. As my Mama told me, you gotta kiss a lot of frogs!

Girl's nights and dinners with friends were so important to me and building me up again. I cherished those times with my friends. Friends are so important to have. Even in a good marriage you have to have healthy time apart. I was alienated from my friends. I will never do that again. One night out with friends I learned a little piece of info that would have been nice to hear many years ago. As we were having wine and hashing out life's most funny and interesting moments, a friend I've had for many years told me something that blew my mind. She had been a mutual friend of mine and Ken's. Her loyalty was certainly to Ken at that time of our lives but she had switched sides after seeing for herself sides of Ken that she didn't like. She very casually says to me that a friend of hers and Ken made out on the night of my bridal shower. What?! Did I hear that right? I shook my head and told her that would have been nice to know at the time. The surprises kept coming. What more had I missed? I wasn't really hurt by it because the healing was well underway and I don't blame that friend for not telling me. God had a plan. As bad as that friend felt for not telling me, I consoled her and said it wasn't her fault.

I continued my therapy in California. I found a therapist that I grew to love. She was actually almost 90 years old! She was a fantastic, foul-mouthed lady who told it like it was. She had been through some trauma herself. She helped me continue to deal with the past and work on a better future for myself. She also taught me so many little tricks to deal with those panic attacks that I was still having. It was all about distraction. If talking to yourself didn't work then distract your mind with something else. Chewing gum and always having a bottle of water were two of my favorite tricks. Singing songs or reciting poems were others, too but when you use those in public, you kinda start to look a little crazy. It was important to me to get through this without any kind of prescription drugs. My therapist was all for giving me whatever prescriptions I wanted. I kept Xanax but it mostly made me tired and I only used it for emergency situations. I don't think it was the easiest way by any means but it was my choice. That wonderful therapist of mine passed away before I could have my last appointment with her.

    Just as life seemed to be finding its new grooves we are hit with another bad piece of information. My Mama was diagnosed with endometrial cancer. Really? Cancer again? Did we have to fight this battle again? The thing about cancer and what I have learned through my Daddy and his massive amounts of research is: cancer loves a body that is dealing with stress! So stop stressing! Easy to say, I know but we all truly have to find peace and remove ourselves from stressful situations. For the sake of our health! I don't want to say I blame myself for my Mama's cancer but I really feel that the stress that she experienced from my life played a part in her cancer. I will never do that to her or my Daddy ever again. The good news is that she had a hysterectomy removing the cancer and she is cancer free to this day!

What Now

It seemed that everywhere I went someone had some new piece of information for me. And it wasn't anything I wanted to hear more about.

I went to visit some old friends in Sacramento. We used to work together. They knew Ken very well. Our kids were the same age so I thought it would be fun to reconnect. As the kids played, we adults had wine and talked. We laughed about old times and cried about others. I had always been fond of this couple. Eyes open now, they had the kind of marriage I had wished I had. They loved each other through and through. They had disagreements but could solve them and learn from them. On that visit I told them how much I idolized their marriage and thanked them for being so great. The wife all of a sudden got tears in her eyes and said she had to tell me something important. For one second it scared me but then something inside me told me exactly what she was going to say. She asked me if I remembered what we were talking about when I had first gotten there on Friday. I remembered a lot of things but nothing stood out. She said, "Remember when you mentioned going to Vegas for your birthday and you said that you were supposed to see Barbie and she never connected with you?" I said, "Yes, why?" She sat there, still with tears in her eyes. She stayed quiet as to give me time to come to the conclusion on my own. I said, "What happened? Did something happen between her and Ken?" The tears started flowing. She started to explain and her husband jumped in, "What are you doing? Why are you doing this now?" She jumped up and told her husband that I deserved to know. If I thought she was a real friend, then I needed to know the truth. I asked her, "How long have you known?" She said that she knew about the time that it had happened. "What?" I said. "Why didn't anyone tell me? How did I not know?" She kept saying how sorry she was that she had not told me. I told her that I understood. Her husband was like a boss to Ken back then and she couldn't get involved even though we were friends.

I told her it was ok. I was alright. There was just one thing I needed to do. Barbie was one of the weather girls at Ken's station when he worked there. I can't really remember how we became friends but back then we were great friends. I trusted her. Nobody else seemed to but I did. Especially the other wives. I felt like the wives were jealous because she was pretty and skinny. I guess maybe they picked up on something that I didn't. Obviously. Barbie and I had kept in touch over the years after she left the station. Most recently, I was going to Vegas, where she now worked and I was hoping to see her. She had flaked on me big time and I found it very strange. I guess now I know why. I sent this Facebook message to her…

You are a disgrace to women. I know you slept with my husband. How dare you. I can't believe I trusted you. I hope you can live with yourself and that you are one of the many. Don't ever contact me. We are done. You disgust me.

Crazy enough she wrote back and tried to deny it calling me mean, childish and disrespectful. I told her that was laughable and what a disappointment she was. I sent Ken a text message asking him about Barbie and the accusations. He didn't deny it one bit. He said that it was terrible of him to do and that he was sorry. I responded by telling him that the worst part was that he allowed me to continue to be friends with her. I still don't know exactly when and what happened and at this point I didn't care. It didn't ruin me or take me to a bad place. The worst was certainly over and learning about yet another indiscretion, even with a friend, didn't bother me too much. Another sign that I had come so far in my healing. I was moving on. Easy. You know what I've learned?

Stupid liars do stupid things. She was a beauty queen, too. Hmmmmm. I deleted her off of Facebook and out of my phone. Goodbye and good riddance.

To this day I really don't know how many times he cheated on me. There was a time that I would walk into a room with him, all eyes on Ken and me, and all I wanted to do was stand on a chair just like Julia Roberts did in the movie Something To Talk About. "Has anyone else here slept with my husband?" I don't even think about it anymore. If you're reading this and know of any, do me a favor…KEEP IT TO YOURSELF!

Out Of The Woodworks

Funny thing when you become single, they all come at you from all different directions. They all have pretty much the same thing to say, "I have always loved you and now I get my chance." Whatever! They tell you everything you want to hear, don't back it up with any action and then you wonder what happened. They chew you up and spit you out and somehow they end up the victim. Something I've noticed with most of these kinds of guys is that they have an unhealthy, way too close relationship with their mothers. As if their mothers wanted to be their friends or maybe perhaps even like partners to their sons. Pretty sick. That is for sure something I have vowed to never be to my boys. I always want to be there for them but as their mother, not their friend. I mean I should have learned with my ex mother-in-law and her relationship with Ken. Now that's an unhealthy one right there!

What was it about these late thirties, early fourties guys, no kids, never been married? Commitment issues? Set in their ways? There is a reason they are still single and you are not going to be the one to change them! I had to do my best to steer clear of them. All of them! But I didn't. I learned my lesson the hard way. It was a new world for me this dating thing. I tried them all. I went a little crazy being single but I was discovering myself. I was figuring out just what kind of guy I really wanted. And I definitely had fun. It was a time in my life that needed to happen. Those times are for another book! I am absolutely grateful for the experiences.

I even had a close call with an old friend who claimed to be separated from his wife. I had met him back in the day when I was just going to college. He was studying broadcast journalism as well. He reached out to me and said those same things. "I have always thought you were beautiful but you were always married." He lived in NYC and was fairly famous now. He traveled a lot for work and wanted to meet up. We flirted and talked about him flying me to see him. It went on for a couple of months when one day I found myself on the other end of something I never wanted to be apart of. There was a message on my phone from him when I woke up one morning but it wasn't from him it was from his wife! He hadn't been separated at all. They were very much still together! My heart sank and I lit him up and ripped him a new one! How dare you do that to me considering all I had been through! There are psychos everywhere and the lesson here was that most of them seemed to be in the news business!

Time To Get Down To Business

The next couple of months seemed to be focused on getting custody and alimony set. It was nice having Ken so far away. Every trip he did make out to California, I dreaded seeing him. It took awhile but I finally stopped being afraid. I still kept up nice always for the sake of the boys. I had been such a good actress for so long. I would probably be good at it forever.

Our first court date was finally upon us. Ken would give me money here and there but it was never stable. He loved still having control over me. My main focus was making sure that the boys were doing well and adjusting to this new life of ours. I looked for jobs that allowed me to pick up the boys after school but nothing seemed worth it. My parents were adamant about all of us getting acclimated to our new life away from Ken and from Florida. I'm so thankful for their patience.

I was so nervous for that day in court. Ken was in Florida so he would have to make his appearance over the phone. My mom was there with me but when my case was called it was just me up at that Plaintiff's table all alone. Everything seemed to go fairly smoothly. The judge ordered the child support and alimony at the standard guideline. That's all I wanted. I just wanted it to be fair. At the end of our time with the judge Ken mentioned that he wanted it noted that he was looking into jurisdiction in Florida. What? The boys and I lived in Florida just a year and a half. That place was not our home. Certainly not the boys' home. Not even Ken's home! He had a timeline to file by so we would just have to see if this was just a threat or if he would follow through.

Christmas came and I had no money. My parents were amazing and made an awesome Christmas for my boys. I really didn't care one bit about the money. I only wanted to be able to take care of the boys and myself and somehow repay my parents for all of their help. If it weren't for them, we would have been homeless. Ken's family knew how much we were struggling and how much my parents were providing for us but they didn't help us one bit. It seemed their money must have been going to help Ken bury me in legal papers and lawsuits.

On Christmas Eve I was served legal papers stating that Ken was trying to get our divorce and custody moved to Florida. What!? I threw up my hands and just started to cry. My mom said, "Well even from Florida he can ruin Christmas!" At that moment all we could do is laugh! I knew this would be another fight but I had done nothing wrong and we would just have to see how it all turned out. We couldn't worry about it.

It took what seemed to be forever for child support and alimony to kick in. Our court date had been in October 2012 but it wasn't until January 2013 that I saw a dime. Since he had not paid me consistently or much at all, the judge ordered hefty arrears and also allowed for me to file a garnishment order to make absolutely sure that the boys and I would get our money. As soon as I started receiving support I was able to contribute to groceries, buy clothes for these growing boys and I started to save for our future!

With every little victory there seemed to be a small defeat. Just as soon as I started receiving money, there was a knock at the door. It was a repo guy who wanted to take my car. I'm sure this guy has seen his share of deadbeats but for some reason he was completely decent to me. He said that my car was on his list since it hadn't been paid in over 3 months. That means Ken had stopped paying for it even before our court date. No surprise there. He told me that he had been watching me and knew that I had kids and didn't want to see me stranded. He gave me 2 days to work it out and agreed to meet me and take my car on that 2nd day. Wow! I was so grateful! Ken obviously didn't care for our well-being. I scrambled to find a car for me and the boys. Luckily dealers see Alimony and Child Support as income so I found a car and thanked the repo guy for his decency. It actually felt so good to have my own bills to pay!

    Time had come to see if the courts would side with Ken and not grant our divorce in California. I wasn't sure exactly why he had pulled this move. I mean California was a no-fault state meaning that it doesn't matter why the marriage breaks up. Money is money and they have a formula for both alimony and child support. But in Florida, the judge can decide alimony and child support based on the reasons for the marriage ending. All of Ken's indiscretions would have surely buried him in Florida. My guess would be that he was trying to look like a father that was fighting for his children. But he wasn't. He was fighting me because he was mad at me for not being under his control anymore. I will never forget that day. My Mama came with me as support but when it was my turn to be heard it was just me all alone at that Plaintiff's table. Ken was in Florida so he was appearing by phone again. The judges in Florida and California would both speak over the phone in judges chambers. We did not hear their conversation. When the judge came back into the courtroom he stated his findings. He said that since I had previously filed for divorce in the state of California and that California was the home of record for the children that it only made sense that California is where all decisions would be made. I couldn't believe it! I was so happy! That nightmare of custody, alimony and child support had been decided! It was an amazing feeling and an awesome victory for me and my boys!

Life Goes On

I was finding my strength in moments of crisis and realized that I was making my way without Ken. The boys were doing great in school. We had a nice routine down and life was going on. Now I'm not gonna say it was a sunshine and rainbows living with my parents but it was a walk in the park compared to the life I used to have. My Mama worked all day so my Daddy was home all the time. We are both very stubborn people and we like to be heard. This was the cause of some fairly heated arguments between my Daddy and me. It was hard for me as a grown woman to live with my parents and it was hard for my Daddy who would always see me as his baby girl. I also believe it was my Daddy's frustrations with the situation at hand. He couldn't kill Ken as I'm sure he would have loved to do! He used every talk we would have as a lesson and I didn't want to hear it. Looking back I can absolutely appreciate where he was coming from and I love him to pieces for his passion and love for me and my boys.

On weekends when Ken would come to visit I would go out with my girlfriends. I had dated here and there but nothing serious and I was ok with that. I had a lot of life to live and I was living it! I also did a lot of stuff just the boys and me. It was scary being alone. The funny part of that statement was that I had been alone for most of my marriage. I likened it to having a tall warm body around. Ken had made me feel useless but the reality was that I knew how to do a lot. It became that the only thing that truly made me nervous being the only adult around was the fear that maybe I couldn't open a tight jar or something! It was an empowering feeling for sure! Just like taking my boys on a vacation to the river with friends. I felt a little out of place since I was the only one there without a husband but the other wives and husbands made me feel very comfortable. It was a great experience except for the fact that I broke my pinky finger while playing football. Oh well. A souvenir of my first vacation alone with my boys.

    We had been living with my parents for almost a year and it was almost time for me and my boys to get a place of our own! It was incredibly exciting but scary. I had always wanted to live at the beach but I wasn't ready to make that move just yet. I figured the right transition for all of us was to get our own place but have it be close to my parents still. So in July of 2013, the boys, our doggy and I moved into our very own home! We found a cute little place in a gated community just down the street from a friend of mine and her husband and kids. It was safe and the kids had friends in the neighborhood. I remember the day I got the keys to that house. I walked through the house, well I skipped through the house. I had nothing to fill it with but it was ours. I first bought us beds. The only things I had taken from our house in Florida were our clothes, kids' toys and a few small pieces of furniture. I knew I didn't want any of that stuff in Florida. Why would I want those memories? Plus I couldn't afford to send much of anything back to California. It was another step in this new life of mine and I was so happy and safe.

As my life seemed to really be taking shape I met a guy who made me laugh and feel beautiful and made me feel safe. We will call him Eric. Eric was a successful, handsome, man in his late thirties, never married, no kids. Oops! Red flag! I fell for Eric hard and fast. He did, for me, too. He lived by the beach so every chance I got I would come down to see him. He would come to my house once in a great while. He met the boys after about 3 months of dating. I wanted to be sure of my feelings before I got them involved. He told me constantly that anyone who knows him, knows that he's not like this. He doesn't date a girl with kids and he certainly doesn't hang out with the kids. He told me things were different with me. We had lots of good times. At first he didn't really know how to be a boyfriend. When it was my birthday he didn't get me a gift or even a card. I had to explain to him that it was important to me, probably important to most girls, that they get at least a card. He truly heard me and felt sorry for that. The next week I dropped and cracked my phone so he bought me a new one. At Christmas he happily bought presents. I did, too but couldn't afford much.

I did what I could for him. He was so busy and such a workaholic that I would love to clean his apartment for him, make sure his fridge was stocked and made him yummy dinners. It was all on the weekends, of course. We lived more inland and my job was as Mama so my weeks were spent with the kids and every other weekend with him. We really didn't talk too much during the week. I missed him but I didn't get that feeling from him. I started to bring up things like the future. He would tell me, "I don't like to think too far ahead." I guess that a single guy with no kids can think that way. I'm sorry but I couldn't. I had kids and I wanted to find someone that wanted to be around all of us. He did take me home back East for a wedding he was attending. It was a lot of fun meeting his friends and seeing where he came from. Everyone told me that he never did this with anyone. That gave me more hope that maybe I would be the one for Eric. Not so fast.

My divorce was final in October of 2013. It felt sad but so good to have that chapter over. Ken called me to see if I was ok after I had text him the news that it had been finalized. I asked him to just do his best at being a father and do better in his next marriage. Oh did I forget to mention? He married the beauty queen! He was officially someone else's problem now.

Step Back

I had been gearing up to move to the beach for the year that we lived in our new house. It was my dream and I wanted to get my boys settled into a new school and district before they were too comfortable. It was then that Ken informed me that he had been let go from his job in Florida. He told me this in May of 2014. In just three weeks he would have no salary. There would be no more child support, no more alimony, no nothing. I scrambled to figure out what to do. I had to give notice at my house and we would have to move back in with my parents. It felt like a huge step back. Luckily I had some savings and knew that it wouldn't be forever.

It was so frustrating how Ken wanted to see me struggle. He knew long before that he wasn't going to have a job. To this day I don't know if he somehow screwed up again or if they were just tired of him in Florida. It was his plan to move back to California with his new bride and find a job out here. I didn't like the idea of having him that close but at least the boys would have more normal visits with him instead of the big events they became when he would come to town.

I knew this was God's way of kicking me in the pants and saying it was time to really take full control of your life. I sent out resume's constantly. I had different resume's for different types of jobs. I got licensed to do eyelash extensions to further my esthetician career. I applied for anything and everything. But nobody wants to hire someone who hasn't had a job outside of the home for many years! I found an employment website where I took on some odd jobs. I did personal assistant work, errands, whatever. You name it, I did it.

    I thought that I hit the jackpot when I interviewed to be in charge of getting a multi-million dollar mansion ready to be sold. The hourly pay was great and it would allow me to stay on track and move to the beach! When I showed up for work that Monday morning, the woman who hired me gave me clothes to change into and told me to put my hair in a bun. There was no way I could have misconstrued what was to be expected of me. I was an organizational specialist, not a housekeeper! But a housekeeper I became. The money was too good and I couldn't pass it up. I was getting absolutely no child support from Ken and I was the sole provider for my boys. So from 8am-5pm with a half hour break for lunch, that's what I did. I cleaned this 5000 square foot house meticulously for this crazy woman.

One morning I had to get the boys enrolled in their new school so I told her that I would be an hour late. I gave her plenty of notice. That weekend she fired me via text to say that it wasn't working out. Without any warning I was now out a job and supposed to be moving in a few weeks. What would I do? I started scouring the website again and was lucky to get another client and then another and then another. Getting fired from that job was the best thing that happened to me.

The move to the beach was scary but successful! The boys started their new school and loved it. I was working many different jobs! It was when I took on a family friend's organizational project that I figured out what I wanted and needed to do! It was then that I decided I would start my own business. I had four different clients that I did regular work for. I was making money. Not great money but good money. I was getting the bills paid and I was proud of myself for doing it on my own.

Ken didn't have a job but was receiving unemployment. The judge ordered for him to pay me $100 per month and he didn't even do that. It was silly to get a garnishment for $100 a month so I stuck it out and hoped he would someday pay for his kids.

I tried calling my Mama one morning as I did just about every day. She didn't answer but just a few minutes later, my Daddy was calling me. I immediately felt that sense that something was wrong. I answered the phone, "What? What's wrong?" My Daddy said, "Everything is fine baby, we are all fine." He then told me that my Mama had woken up yesterday morning and couldn't feel her right side. Yesterday? This happened yesterday and you are just telling me now!? I was so mad at my parents because they kept it from me. They didn't want me to worry until they knew what it was to worry about. My Daddy was being his usual funny self even after it was diagnosed as a stroke. He would say, "I've got the pen ready for her to hold in her hand!" As if to say she was like Bob Dole. Oh my Daddy. But it sure made us all laugh! Laughter is definitely the best medicine.

My Mama was so frustrated with her recovery. She wanted everything back right away. She worked her butt off in therapy and at home. The only real sign left of the stroke is it's hard for her to pick up small items with her fingers. It still makes her mad to this day but an amazing recovery she made!

Living at the beach I was closer to my boyfriend Eric. Funny thing was, we saw each other just as much as we did before. I started to realize that Eric only wanted an escape on the weekends. And it was an escape for, me, too. We drank and partied a lot together but when it came down to it, that was all that we had. I had a serious talk with him one night and he said he needed time to think things over. It would be hard for me but I would give him that time.

Two weeks went by and neither him nor I reached out to each other. Before the big talk had happened I had been planning a surprise birthday party for him. I spoke to a mutual friend of ours about whether I should still go through with the party or not and she gave me a slight indication that she seemed to know more than me about where Eric's head was at. I called him and told him I was coming over and this was getting ridiculous. When I got to Eric's apartment, he treated me like a crazy person. Like he had already come to the conclusion that it was over and I was just supposed to know that. What? I was giving you time and space buddy! It was a sad realization that my year and a half with Eric was over. For some reason it was such a hard breakup to take. My heart was broken again. I couldn't be what he wanted either. I had seen a future with Eric but he didn't see one with me.

It took me what seemed like forever to get over Eric. The timing sucked because it was right around Christmas. We were supposed to be spending his birthday and Christmas together. It was difficult but after 2 weeks I was doing much better. My friends called me every day to cheer me up and to take me out. I actually started to love my alone time, too. It was learning to embrace being alone and happy with me where I found myself again. I was able to open myself to all of the right things…and people!

Ken finally had a new job which finally meant some child support! I had been fully supporting my boys without the help of anyone for a year and a half! He didn't give me a dime! So when he got his new job, I was quick to ask him for support. He gave me a copy of his new contract. It wasn't a lot but I was happy to be getting any kind of help! I shouldn't have trusted so easily here but that is a lesson to be learned later. We came up with an agreement, signed it and filed it with the court. He promised that there didn't need to be a garnishment order. He showed me how he had done a direct deposit request and that the money would go directly into my account. Like

I said, I was happy to be getting support now so I went with it. Just 2 months after he started paying support he pulled the direct deposit and I was left with nothing. I had to get a garnishment order which took 2 months to kick in. He hasn't changed one bit and he never will.

A Perfect Match

After I had healed from my breakup with Eric and had been alone for about a month, I thought it was time to start dating again. My Mama and I were sitting at their house together having some wine and discussing just how I get back into the dating world. I had gotten an email from match.com about a free trial and wanted to see what she thought about that. She said "Go for it!" So right then and there I signed up. I was filling in all the important information. My likes and dislikes. My criteria for a guy. It was fun! When I questioned my own response on something my Mama said, "This is the man of your dreams you don't need to skimp." She was right. If I was going to do this it had to be everything I ever wanted. As I posted my picture and officially signed on, we both giggled. I had no real expectations at all. It was just another adventure in this life of mine.

I think that it is important to learn and believe that you can have it all. When you are controlled and abused for so long you can adapt to anything. You can tell yourself that it is fine and be ok with it. But it doesn't have to be fine. It doesn't have to be ok. What is it that you really want? What do you want your life to be? I realized that I had not only settled in my life with Ken but I had done it again in my relationship with Eric. He was certainly a step up for Ken. He would never hurt me emotionally or physically but he wasn't everything I wanted or needed either. I wanted a guy who saw me as his partner in life. I wanted a partner who wanted to make plans with me. It was hard getting Eric to commit to even a weekend away together let alone a life together! Eric was very clear that he was his own man and loved his bachelor lifestyle. It's important to remember that actions speak louder than words. Guys will tell you so much of what you want to hear which is always still hard for me because I am honest. I don't understand the idea of lying. But pay attention to the actions and not the words. They will tell you everything you need to hear. I know Eric loved me as much as he was capable of, but that was not enough for me. It was good enough at the time, but I wanted something forever and I wasn't going to settle again.

Taylor and I made a pact that we wouldn't even give our number out to another guy unless he had everything we really wanted in a husband. A husband. Not just another guy to date.

My first glimpse of Kurt was when he "Favorited" me. In Match language that's when someone views your profile and adds you to their favorite list. I remember squealing with delight when that popped up in my notifications. I of course, had to get a look at this guy. By the looks of him, he was totally my type. He was cute. Brown hair, brown eyes, professional looking. He was wearing a tie in his profile pic. Now when I read his profile I was blown away. He said everything I wanted in a guy. He said he wanted to find the one to spend his golden years with. He wanted a partner in life to love and to laugh with. Could this guy be real? So I decided to "Wink" at him. He had already put me on his favorites list so I thought that was ok. Within a few minutes, Kurt had sent me a message. We messaged back and forth that night till after 1 in the morning.

He gave me his phone number and we started to text the next day. I talked to a couple of guys on there one or two times but no one could compare to what I was already feeling and my connection with Kurt. It was a holiday weekend and I was visiting my parent's so we decided that we would have our first date on that next Wednesday night.

I can't even tell you how nervous and excited I was for that first date with Kurt. We had been texting that whole first part of the week. We had even talked on the phone to get that part out of the way. We decided that we would meet near his house and walk to a restaurant in the area. I had expressed my concerns for safety and that I was nervous about that. He said that he had never met anyone off of Match and had them at his home. We were on the same page. He text and told me where to park. He was waiting on the street when I drove up. A good sign. I got out of the car and he opened my door for me. He was super cute and smelled good. We just sort of aimlessly starting walking and we ended up in his apartment. I even said, "Ummm I'm in your place." He laughed and couldn't believe it either. There was something special about him but I wasn't gonna get my hopes up just yet. Be realistic.

We walked to a nearby restaurant. Conversation was easy and comfortable. I learned he was from Washington state and had moved here after a divorce and a new start in paradise. We had very similar situations. The night was going so well. After dinner, we started on our walk back to Kurt's place. I wasn't sure about how he felt about holding hands just yet so I grabbed his arm. Kurt started talking about how he's been told that this time of year you can see the plankton light up in the waves. I knew exactly what he was trying to do but I let him convince me to take a walk near the sand so we could check it out. There was no plankton but there was a great first kiss! That night we went back to his place and talked and kissed all night. Kurt had to be up at 3:45am for work but he didn't care. We knew right away this was something special. We dozed off and then Kurt's alarm went off. I left to let him get ready for work. I went home, put my pajamas on and went to sleep.

After that first date we were inseparable. There was just something about him that I couldn't describe. I was so comfortable when I was with him. After just a week of dating I told my mom that I was going to marry Kurt! That same week, Kurt told me that he was falling in love with me. I introduced him to the boys very quickly, but when you know, you know. The boys could see the excitement that their Mama was feeling and they couldn't wait to meet this guy! I remember the first night I stayed over at his house, I was actually able to sleep! I slept well and felt safe and sound.

What Kurt said, he did. He is a real man. He had nothing to hide. He would say everything that was on his mind. And sometimes more than I wanted to know. But there were no secrets. Trust was huge for him as it was for me. He did things that I never even realized I wanted. He opened my door and not just the door to the restaurant but my car door. He walked on the busy side of the street. And to the side of me, holding my hand. Not 3 feet in front of me. He didn't even drink coffee but he made me mine and he brought it to me in bed. And he did this every single day. I don't know how many times I said to him, "When are you going to change?" He wasn't going to change. He was real and he wanted to be with me forever.

My therapist in Florida always told me when I did start to date that you can usually tell who someone really is after 6 months of dating. She said by then, all of the best behavior has probably worn off and they are who they are. I had told Kurt that and he would joke, "Has it been 6 months yet, I am sick of faking it." He could always make me laugh. He was so charming but real. He was a smart business man but he knew how to turn it off and focus on me. On us. I loved hearing him talk on business phone calls. He was so good at what he did. More importantly, he was so good at loving me. He made me feel loved and sexy every day. Just about every single day I get a text from him at some point in his busy day that says, "I love you baby." I never imagined how much I would love to hear someone call me baby. Or he would send a completely inappropriate text, too! He made me feel wanted and I loved him for it.

After just 6 months of dating, Kurt popped the question right there in the same spot where we shared our first kiss. I called my best friend the next day to tell her I was engaged and she already knew. Kurt knew how important Taylor's opinion was to me. Taylor said the day before Kurt had sent her a picture of the ring and told her that he was going to ask me. She started to cry and so did I. She was so overwhelmed with joy that I had indeed found the man of my dreams. He would love me like I had always wanted and deserved. Kurt had also asked both of my parents for their permission. He listened to me and he wanted what was best for me.

Trusting someone is so hard, even when they are the real deal. The one thing I absolutely know about Kurt is that he would never cheat on me. He doesn't even look at other girls. I am always telling him, "It's ok to look honey, just don't touch." But he doesn't want any part of either. I tried a couple of times not to believe he was real. I tried to push him away. I believed every man would betray me. I thought every guy cheats. I tried to sabotage this amazing relationship I had found. But Kurt wasn't going anywhere. He stuck through those tough moments. He worked with me. He knew my pain and what I had been through. When we would have fights, he would never lay a hand on me. Never. He is a real man and that's what real men do. They stay and they do the work. They love you through it. I looked at a list of things I wanted in a man that I had written down just two years before…

-kisses me every time he comes home
-once in awhile, makes and brings me coffee
-takes out the trash
-helps to clean up after dinners and parties
-makes plans with me far in advance
-asks me how my day was
-wants to marry me someday
-wants to be a big part of the boys lives
-brings me flowers once in awhile
-always fills my glass
-wants to grow old with me
-wants to cuddle at night and in the morning
-can keep up with my drive
-wants to stay active and eat healthy
-cares about my overall well-being
-tells me I look nice without me having to ask
-thinks about me and wants to make decisions together

-will wake me up if I fall asleep on the couch
-will be supportive of my dreams
-will be sensitive to my fragile heart
-will always speak to me respectfully, even in a fight. No name calling.
-will never lay a hand on me
-AND THE SAME APPLIES TO ME!

Finally, I realized he's one of the good guys. He does all of those things and more! I let all of my walls down and fully let him in. He is the love of my life, my true partner. He's the one I want to grow old with and make plans with and live the best years of my life with. He's the one I want to make babies with! Or at least try our hardest to! And you know what? He feels the exact same way about me! Actually when I tell him I love him, without fail he says, "I love you more." He is a great dad to his kids and a great step-dad to my boys. I have the family I have always wanted. It's not at all how I envisioned it but God did.

We always wished we had met each other sooner, but our age difference was probably a huge factor in that. Kurt is almost 9 years older, plus the fact that he had lived in Washington, but God had a plan and this would be the time for our happily ever after. Everything truly fell into place for us. We got an amazing deal on a house just steps from the sand. My business took off and so did his. We had our wedding at our home. We are blessed and grateful.

And So It Goes

Ken never ceases to amaze me. You would think since he's living the life that he wants, he would have some peace and goodness in it. He has the wife that he has always wanted and a new baby girl. He has a great job. He has 2 beautiful boys. It sounds like life would be awesome. But he still has to be devious.

After I got married to Kurt, Ken and I were finalizing our newest support order. No longer would there be alimony so we were just hashing out child support. Funny thing is not once has he ever asked for more time with them. It's always just about the money.

As I was filing these documents that we had agreed upon I was at the Help Center making sure I was filling everything out right. The girl at the Help Center asked me one simple question, "Did you get his contract from him or the company?" I gave her a funny look and said, "Him." She suggested that I get a subpoena for his contract and employment records from his company just to be sure he was telling the truth. I did just that and wouldn't you know it, he was lying!? I mean not just by a little but by double! He actually makes double what he told me! A lie that would cost him dearly.

The judge would order him to pay me arrears in the 5 digits! He ripped Ken a new one for what he had done. He even said that Ken was lucky I wasn't asking for sanctions or jail time! Wait, what? I could do that?! That was all for falsifying his contract and lying about it for a year and a half! It was so great to have someone finally put him in his place. He isn't above it all and rules do apply to you buddy! And you can bet I got a garnishment order for all of it! It constantly seems to be a control issue with him. His lack of control over me still fuels him. I am nobody's possession. I am me and no one will change me ever again.

My life is not perfect now by any means, but damn close to what I imagine perfect to be. I never take anything for granted. In fact that is something that I am still working on. I do worry when this is all going to change? When is this beautiful new reality of mine going to be taken away from me? It's not. It's mine and God has blessed me. I cherish everything. I have the scars from a life that used to be mine. But I also have lessons that I learned. I have no regrets. Some decisions I have made were not the best but I survived. I wake up every day grateful to God with a smile on my face, (well almost everyday) ready to attack the day for whatever life brings.

My boys are doing so amazing. I protect them just the right amount. They will know in time just how far I have come. I know they are on their way to becoming great men thanks to their step-dad. Both of them take out the trash and open doors for the women around them. They have sweet hearts and smart minds. I am so proud. I have an awesome husband who is completely devoted to me and my boys. He lets me, be me. He laughs at me when I feel like dancing and being silly. And he listens to me when I'm having a hard time. I mean there truly is nothing sexier than a man who loves his wife, right? He loves me for all of me, even the bad parts. But he knows that without all of it, I would never be who I am today. And today I can say that I like me. I love me.

Made in the USA
San Bernardino, CA
23 October 2017